ANEW

*Living Life As A
Better You*

SHYRA SMITH

Copyright © 2023 Shyra Smith

All Rights Reserved. No part of this book may be reproduced in any form without permission from the author or publisher, except as permitted by U.S. copyright law. To request permission, contact *shyra@shyrasmith.com*

This publication is designed to provide researched and authoritative information in regard to the subject matter covered. It is sold with the understanding that neither the author or publisher is engaged in rendering any medical or professional advice or services. While the publisher and author have used their best efforts in preparing this book, they make no representations or warranties with respect to the accuracy or completeness of the contents of this book and specifically disclaim any implied warranties of merchantability or fitness for a particular purpose. No warranty may be created or extended by sales representatives or written sales materials. The advice and strategies contained herein may not be suitable for your situation. You should consult with a professional when appropriate. Neither the publisher nor the author shall be liable for any loss profits or any other commercial damages, including but not limited to special, incidental, consequential, personal, or other damages.

While the author and publisher have made every effort to provide accurate internet addresses at the time of publication, neither the author or publisher assumes any responsibility for errors, or for any changes that may occur after publication. Further, the publisher nor author have any control over and does not assume any responsibility for third-party websites or their content.

ISBN paperback: 979-8-9897560-0-1
ISBN e-book: 979-8-9897560-1-8
ISBN hardcover: 979-8-9897560-2-5

Printed in United States of America

Published by HS3 Enterprises,
1301 E. Debbie Lane, Ste. 102-137
Mansfield, Texas 76063

Learn more about Shyra Smith at *www.shyrasmith.com*

TABLE OF CONTENTS

Introduction: "Be Transformed by the Renewing of Your Mind" 5
    First, Think About Your Thoughts 10
    Seek Direction 11
    Accept the Challenge 11

Part 1 13
Chapter 1: Hello, I Was You 15
Chapter 2: "Everything in Adulthood Can be Traced Back to Childhood" — Penny Junor 29
    What Are Adverse Childhood Experiences? 32
    Is One Adverse Childhood Experience Worse Than Another? 34
Chapter 3: You Are Not Fine, Not Really 41
    How We Are Affected by Unresolved ACEs 41
    Physical Effects of ACEs in Adults 42
    Psychological Effects of ACEs on Adults 45
    Spiritual Effects: How the Devil Uses Our Trauma Against Us 48
    You Need to Stop Sinking Your Boat 52
Chapter 4: Do You Believe the Thought Makes the Person? ... 55
    Sources of Limiting Beliefs 58
    Effects of Limiting Childhood Beliefs in Our Adult Lives 64
Chapter 5: Your Grandma's Fine China Is Not The Only Thing You Inherited 67
    Hidden Generational Patterns and How They Affect Us 71

King David and His Sons (2 Samuel 11, 12, 13,
& 14, NIV) (1 Kings 11 & 12, NIV) 71
Rebecca and Jacob (Genesis 25, 27, 30, and 37) 74
Chapter 6: It's Not Always Trauma..79
The Parable of the Talents (Matthew 25:14-30, NRSVA) ...84

Part 2 89

Chapter 7: It's Not Your Fault, But It Is
Your Responsibility 91
Recovering from Childhood Trauma:
Let the Healing Begin 94
Steps to Recovering from Childhood Trauma......................94
Chapter 8: Breaking Generational Patterns and Behaviors:
You Are Not Your Parents 105
Become the Cycle Breaker 106
How to Become the Cycle Breaker 109
Chapter 9: Ridding Yourself of Limiting
Childhood Beliefs...119
Write Down Your Beliefs 123
Explore Their Root..124
Recognize Their Effect...125
Uproot and Replant...126
Write Down New Beliefs...127
Chapter 10: Work, Trust, and Obey 131
Work..131
Trust 134
Obey 137
The Wedding Feast at Cana (John 2:1-12) 138
Simon's Many Fishes (Luke 5: 1-11 NIV) 139
Chapter 11: If They Could, So Can You...............................141
Joseph (Genesis 37-50, NIV)...142
Esther (Esther 1-10, NIV) 146
Chapter 12: You Are God's Masterpiece................................153

References 159
Bible References...159
Articles 160

INTRODUCTION

"BE TRANSFORMED BY THE RENEWING OF YOUR MIND"

Imagine this: You're standing at the threshold of every hope, every dream, and everything good you've ever wanted for yourself. Behind that door lies all the things your mother insisted you weren't good enough for and everything your father claimed wasn't meant for someone like you. It holds the affection, love, courage, and worth that your partner may have stolen from you through toxic actions and hurtful words.

Behind that door is a place where your trauma can no longer hurt you, where it no longer dictates the course of your life. There is light behind that door, along with success, growth, truth, and unconditional love. It's a place where your experiences and triumphs become an inspiration to others, where generational patterns and family wounds are shattered. It's a place where you are no longer constrained by society's limits on what you can and can't achieve.

You are free, you are thriving, and you are loved. You are not broken; instead, your cracks have been mended, creating a unique, beautiful pattern of renewal and growth. You are living your best life, the life that God intended for you all along.

This door stands right in front of you, beckoning, waiting for you to turn the knob and step into the life that is rightfully yours. But you hesitate. Why? Because you can't see it. Even though your eyes are wide open, your mind remains closed. Instead of this beautiful, conspicuous door, you see a web of lies, half-truths, empty platitudes, and negativity, all entwined in a cycle of toxic thoughts.

These thoughts have convinced you that you cannot become anything more than what you are right now. They are the lies that have been imposed on you about your identity and potential. They are the half-truths that have clouded your understanding. And they are the empty words that have lost their true meaning. But everything you need for transformation awaits just beyond that door. You need only to step out of the cycle of your old thoughts and embrace the challenge of renewing your mind.

How? The apostle Paul said it best: *Do not conform to the pattern of this world, but be transformed by the renewing of your mind. Then you will be able to test and approve what God's will is—His good, pleasing and perfect will* (Romans 12:2, NIV).

Does that verse overwhelm you? Does it sound unrealistic? Does it make you want to close this book and continue with your day? You may be thinking, *What pattern is Paul talking about? I don't follow anyone's rules but my own.* So, let's unpack that verse with these questions:

Have you ever considered what God's will for your life is? Has it ever occurred to you that you might be living outside of it? Do you wholeheartedly believe that this is the life you were meant to live, right here and right now?

When Paul wrote that verse to the Romans, he had high hopes for them. You see, they had just become Christians. But before that, throughout their lives, they had conformed to the pattern of the world. They had done what everyone else did, following rules and laws that actually distanced them from God rather than bringing them closer. They had forsaken their identities as children of God in favor of conforming to what the world deemed acceptable. They had been living their lives on autopilot, likely carrying burdens and traumas that prevented them from living as God intended.

So when Paul instructed them not to conform any longer, he meant for them to let go of the old ways. He wanted them to stop being controlled by rules, laws, and ideas that hindered their potential and prevented them from embracing their true selves. His intention was for them to discard what they thought was true and embrace God's truth. Specifically, he wanted them to change their thought patterns, lifestyles, and default habits, believing that this transformation would align them with God's will for their lives.

Much like the Romans, we often spend our lives conforming to "truths" and thoughts that we aren't even consciously aware of. We unknowingly embrace lies imposed on us by fear, family, friends, trauma, obstacles, or influential individuals in our lives. We conform to standards set by social media and content creators who may not understand us or God's purpose for us. We allow adverse circumstances and experiences to dim our joy and obscure our true identities. We've been conforming for too long, allowing the enemy to prevail. Yes, the enemy. Many of these falsehoods originate from him, as he sometimes manipulates those closest to us to undermine us. While conformity has its place, it should never overshadow God's will in your life.

I understand that if you're not a Christian, these verses and lines may make you feel uncomfortable. I get it. However, renewing your mind starts with opening it up to possibilities you hadn't considered before. So, please stay with me.

Our lives consist of patterns, both minor and major habits, thoughts, desires, and decisions that accumulate to form the larger framework of our lives.

The seemingly random decisions you make and the truths you believe all contribute to the life you lead. Although some things may appear random, nothing truly is, because beyond the framework of our lives, we exist within a larger one—one that is controlled and ordained by God.

In God's framework, you must either stand in the identity He has given you and work according to the plans He has laid out, or you will go through life never truly knowing who you are. Which path would you prefer?

To renew your mind and experience transformation, you need to shift your focus. You must start thinking and seeing differently. You need to recognize and accept your true self. You must stop conforming to the outcomes of your trauma and the dictates of society. Many people are currently navigating life with despair, believing their existence is meaningless and they can never be more. But that doesn't have to be your story. Your true life, your best self, will reveal itself once you stop accepting the randomness or apparent pointlessness of things and start embracing the fact that you were created with a unique destiny and truth.

However, before you embark on this journey, you must understand that there is nothing random about your existence or what has happened to you. In 2011, Mel Robbins delivered a TEDx Talk where she revealed that, according to scientists, the odds of you being born in this exact time are one in 400 trillion.

For you to exist, your ancestors had to meet, and their ancestors before them, and so on.

You are not a random occurrence; your existence is not arbitrary, and neither is your trauma. There's a reason, a greater design, always at play. This reason may not make sense to you right now or even years from now, but God knows His plans for you. He sees you, always has, and to truly see Him, to feel Him, and to be guided by His will to the door that holds everything you need, you must be willing to open your mind.

That's where this book comes in. It will take you on a journey that challenges every negative thought you've ever believed, every lie etched into your heart. Think of this book as your guide to a phase of life characterized by peace and self-awareness.

But you can't embark on this journey unless you're prepared for it.

First, Think About Your Thoughts

What are your most frequent recurring thoughts, and why do they persist? What do you believe about yourself, and how did those beliefs take root? The truth is, we often don't consciously consider our thought patterns, but our minds remain active throughout the day, impacting us whether we're aware of it or not. These thoughts influence our actions, and the more attention we give them, the deeper they take root. That's why the first step in renewing your mind is to understand your recurring thought patterns.

Think of your mind as a house in need of renovation. You know there's work to be done, but before you can start, you must thoroughly inspect the house and assess all the damage. By fully recognizing and acknowledging the damage, you can begin the process of repair. Have you taken that step? Or have you become so accustomed to the damage that your trauma has become a distorted version of normalcy?

Seek Direction

Have you ever felt that something was off, something was wrong, but you had no idea what it was? Does your situation feel like an absolute maze? This book contains numerous resources and a wealth of knowledge, but not all of it may apply to you. Even the information that does may not be immediately obvious. So, ask God for guidance, open your heart, and express your readiness to renew your mind. The process of renewing your mind only truly works when you are willing to surrender to a truth more powerful than the lies you've been told.

Accept the Challenge

Throughout your life, you've been conditioned to believe certain things. These beliefs have become deeply ingrained in your subconscious, and unlearning them won't be easy. At times, it might feel like you're trying to fix something that isn't broken. You may even lose friends, and some family members might resent you for it, but that's perfectly fine. Why? Because your true self doesn't require the approval and love of everyone. It won't beg for affection, nor will it contort itself to please others. You need to become the person you're meant to be, and if that entails leaving some people behind, so be it. Your transformation will be beautiful, albeit challenging, and it will take time…but it will indeed be beautiful.

This quote from Watchman Nee, a renowned Chinese evangelist, sums this up beautifully: *If you perform your part, God will fulfill His. And once you put off specifically, you should just as thoroughly believe that God will renew your mind, despite the fact you know not how.*

Okay, let's begin!

PART 1

CHAPTER 1

HELLO, I WAS YOU

It's hard to take advice or counsel from someone who has never been in your shoes. A person who has never felt, and probably will never feel, the weight of the personal trauma you've carried. It's not just hard; it can also feel a bit upsetting. What do they know? How can they possibly understand? Your trauma feels heavy and all-consuming, and this relaxed, soft-spoken person who looks like they've never struggled a day wants to review and discuss your issues and tell you how you can feel better. It can feel ridiculous!

I hear you and I can agree. Isn't it unbelievable how the people who have never experienced the unfortunate experiences you've been through are always quick to give advice? It's like a male doctor telling a woman in labor to suck it up because it can't be that bad. So, before you conclude that this is just another self-help book, I need you to understand that I speak from experience. Every issue we are going to explore in this book is one I've dealt with personally. I understand. I get it because I've been there.

I know what it feels like to be neglected, rejected, and psychologically manipulated (or as it's commonly referred to today, gaslit). I've dealt with a painful and senseless death that sometimes doesn't make sense to me even now. I know that through God and the active renewing of your mind, there's nothing you can't overcome, because I have. I've OVERCOME.

I've learned that the best teachings come from experience, whether yours or someone else's. I also understand that sometimes it can feel as though we're alone or alienated when we go through the tough things in life. I've gone through things that made me feel exactly like that.

But I made a discovery that I want to share with you: You have not been alienated. You've been nominated to go through some of those horrible things that happened to you. It wasn't random; no, you were singled out for it. I've come to believe that God doesn't give us more than we can handle. He has a purpose for each of us and knows our strengths. That's how He knew and trusted I would be strong enough to go through the unfortunate experiences I did, just as He trusts you to go through yours for your purpose so that one day we can lead others out of the wreck of theirs.

Many parents with unresolved trauma can have difficulty providing a healthy upbringing for their children. Stay around a cold, insensitive parent long enough, and you will see the imprint of their childhood trauma all over them.

My mother was not a soft woman, but not by choice. I don't recall her displaying sensitivity or vulnerability. And even when at home, away from everyone, she still didn't extend them to me. For most of my childhood, it felt like I was more of a prop for the image she was trying to project to others, like I was this thing that existed to please and make her proud at the detriment of my needs, potential, or happiness. But this was no fault of hers. You see, I thought my upbringing with my mother was traumatizing, and it was. But the moment I put hers side by side with mine, I saw she could not help being the mother she was. It's true, you cannot give what you don't have, and my mother could not give vulnerability and sensitivity because she never grew up with that. She grew up in a time much different than now, a time when survival trumped vulnerability. When you grow up like that, you believe there is no place for sensitivity in the struggle to live. Sensitivity and vulnerability become luxuries you can't afford.

A good friend of mine died when I was a teenager, at the early start of our summer vacation. My parents had long been divorced by then. Their chaotic divorce was difficult for me as a child, but this was not acknowledged in our household by either parent. They did not talk about it with me as they should have. I was just expected to carry on and act as if everything was normal. But, of course, it wasn't. I was struggling and confused, and I didn't understand why my father suddenly didn't want to live with us anymore.

The last couple of weeks before school had let out for the summer, my friend told me, "You better make time for me this summer… We need to hang out! You better call me!" I was looking forward to hanging out, and I always responded by telling her that I would. In fact, on the very last day of school, I recall promising I would call and let her know when I was back from my dad's house.

A couple of weeks after school was out, I returned from visiting my dad and planned to reach out to my friend the following week. I never got that chance because the day I told myself I would call her was the day she died. It was so random and unexpected, and I was beyond devastated. I didn't understand it.

As an adult, I've learned we have no control over death. When it happens, it happens. And at my age at the time, I really needed help processing that. But I didn't get it.

I had so many sleepless nights, and the one time I ran to my mother's room because I was terrified from a dream I had, she demanded that I go back to my room. She never even opened her bedroom door for me to come in. I remember knocking on her door and just standing there in tears, begging her to let me into her room because I didn't want to be alone. But she didn't. I stood there, feeling rejected, struggling with the pointlessness of my friend's death, and wondering why I couldn't get the support I needed from my mother.

When I began to work on my healing as an adult, I perused article after article, trying to find answers and get an understanding of my mother's behavior. I would discover a list of devastating adverse childhood experiences (ACEs) that matched up to ones I learned that she had encountered growing up. She had lived in an environment where it seemed she was just trying to survive. There was no sympathy, no empathy, no vulnerability or sensitivity. So how could she give what she didn't receive?

As I got older, I started to experience symptoms from my trauma. Symptoms that had me feeling inadequate, insecure, unloved, rejected, invalidated, and guilty at different times in my life. I hated feeling like that, and that's when it hit me: I had been feeling like that the majority of my life. I realized I needed to get to the bottom of what was happening and began to do my own research and work. The words, the symptoms, and the results from the many articles I perused practically jumped out at me. Probably the way they will jump out at you as you read the upcoming chapters. I was not fine, I was not okay, my trauma was eating at me, and I needed a change.

I don't want to go into all of the details of the ACEs I discovered my mother went through as a child and the trauma of it all. And I don't want to go as in depth into mine. That's another book. This book is to help us understand the fact that we had no control over how we were raised. We had no control over the trauma we endured, but we are adults now, and we have a choice on how we handle it. We have a choice to move forward and break the cycle spinning for generations. I did it. Once it became clear to me that I couldn't live how I was anymore, I had to.

I'm familiar with experiencing neglect and emotional abuse. However, the closer I drew to God, the more I began to understand that I didn't have to be defined by that phase in my life. I would never treat my kids the way I was treated because I know better. By choosing to heal, I am, by God's grace, raising kids who will go on to do better with their own kids.

Yes, I get it. I know exactly how it feels to be loved conditionally. Throughout my childhood and into my adult life, it felt like I was there for my mother in ways she wouldn't think to be for me. I felt as if I was loved conditionally, based on what I could do, what I could give, or how I made her look. I felt I had to forgo who I was or what I wanted in favor of my mother in the hopes that she would love me more or not begin to love me less. And many, many times, I did forgo myself, my happiness, and my growth just to get a molecule of love and validation from her.

Growing up like that skewed my idea of love and relationships. It made me see them as transactional because I thought I had to give something to be seen or loved. But when I began to think of God as my real and true Father, as the parent who loved me unconditionally, I began to understand the true meaning of selfless love. And I came to a life-changing realization: I am loved, not for what I can give God—honestly, I couldn't possibly give Him anything to match the love He gives me—but simply because I am.

Have you ever felt extreme confusion? That was me when my parents divorced. I was just a child when it happened, a sensitive one at that. I didn't understand why my father left or why my mother said mean things about him to me. I lived with my mother and visited my dad every other weekend. Some weekends, my dad simply didn't show up. There were no calls, no apologies; he just wasn't there. The first time it happened, I waited in front of the window, looking out until it got dark. I remember wondering where he was and why he wouldn't at least call to let me know he was running late. It was heartbreaking. At that time, it felt like I was just an inconvenience. Years later, as I became old enough to understand the truth about my parents' marriage and their chaotic behaviors even after their marriage, I did what I could to keep the peace—not for their sake, but for mine. It was difficult, and I always felt caught in the middle. If you're a parent using your kids to upset the other parent, please stop. In the long run, you end up hurting your kids, and they WILL eventually learn the truth.

Remember that I mentioned being gaslit? That was me every time I tried to have a healthy conversation with my mother about her hurtful actions that I experienced as a child and eventually as an adult. I recall times when she would respond to me by saying, "It wasn't that bad" or "You're too sensitive." I was even told, "You're just trying to make it sound like I was a bad mother." She would never take responsibility for her actions and many times would continue to turn things around to attempt to make me believe things were my fault. As a kid, this was tough. It caused me to doubt myself at times and be unsure about my feelings.

As a child, I would sometimes bury my feelings for fear of being called oversensitive or overdramatic. And as an adult, with renewed knowledge, it hurt even more because I finally understood it.

My mother saw my sensitivity as a weakness. She also didn't understand my need to discuss or understand why things were the way they were. She didn't understand; there were feelings being hurt. She didn't even understand that she was raising me much like she had been raised.

Many parents gaslight their children when they don't give them the chance to explain how they've been hurt. Some parents still believe they can never be wrong or that they can disrespect or embarrass their kids, even if it risks the child's emotional maturity. How will a child ever learn to own up to their faults or apologize if they never saw their parents do it, either with them or with others? As an adult navigating this, I came to understand it. I grasped where my mother was coming from, but it was still disappointing. I kept waiting for her to own up to her faults, but as of today, it still hasn't happened.

That's one thing I had to accept. My mother may never acknowledge the hurt she caused me. The moment I accepted that, I forgave her and focused on my own healing.

If you've ever had to pretend to be fine when you weren't, that was me every time my mother insisted that I maintain a good image for others on the outside. It was challenging, especially during the early years in elementary school. I despised taking school pictures because you could clearly see how miserable I felt on the inside. There are a couple of photos of me struggling to hold back tears. I never felt nurtured, and the habit of constantly hiding my feelings took a toll on me. Eventually, I realized that projecting a false image—putting on a façade—was essentially lying to myself.

If you're hurt, you should be able to say so. If you're angry, you should be able to express it. Many people endure difficult situations because they never learned to express themselves honestly. They've spent their entire lives maintaining a facade for their own or others' benefit. The image my mother insisted I uphold seemed to serve only her interests. I was hurting because all I wanted was to feel seen and heard by her. As a mom, I encourage my kids to be themselves and never fake an image or pretend to be something they're not, not for me or anyone else.

If you've ever felt guilty or responsible for something you didn't do, that was me throughout my life with my mother. Even as an adult, after getting married, I still felt that restraining chain, the perpetual feeling of never being good enough or not doing enough when it came to her. I couldn't seem to do anything right, and the positive things I did for myself often felt like an offense to her.

My husband would take me and our kids on summer vacations, and I remember a time when she held a grudge and became combative with me because he took us to a place she claimed to have always wanted to visit, and I should have ensured that she went with us. I had to involve her in my life on her terms, regardless of whether it benefited me. She would scrutinize the good things happening in my life with jealousy, effectively stealing the joy from something that should have been a positive aspect of my life. I had to bear the burden of her bitterness, and despite my best efforts to improve things, I continually fell short of her approval.

Many parents have thrived on guilting their children, expecting them to give up something in their life for the parent's own benefit. We are to honor our parents, respect and love them, not bend over backward to please them or be provoked by them. Parents with narcissistic behaviors don't understand this. To them, you are only doing enough when they say you are.

I experienced a mother who criticized and withheld her love, giving it only when it benefitted her.

Creating boundaries with her has been one of my most challenging tasks. However, I did it because I realized that my healing was essential for my well-being and how I would raise my children. That's the risk you run when you don't take the time and effort to heal—you may inadvertently subject your kids and grandkids to the fallout from actions they didn't commit.

When I chose to embark on my healing journey, I prayed frequently and allowed God to guide my steps through it all. I had to unlearn many things and relearn many others, effectively renewing my mind. I couldn't control how I was raised, but as an adult, I had the power to change. I needed to become the person I wanted to be, not just for myself but also for my husband and my children. I couldn't give them a whole me until I had worked on my healing. While I forgave my mother, I had to continue protecting myself from further emotional abuse. I understood that she did the best she could with the knowledge she had when she raised me. Armed with new understanding, I had to move forward and do better.

Do you believe you're trapped in an unbreakable cycle of generational family patterns? That used to be my belief. My feelings always seemed inconsequential, and I was conditioned to cater to my mom's needs. Any deviation in thought or expression of my own opinions was met with criticism or an attempt to make me feel guilty for having my own perspective. I initially thought it was just my mom's behavior, but one day, I overheard my grandmother making similar comments to my mother. I was already an adult with my own children when I witnessed this identical behavior. I watched my mother's demeanor change, and it was like witnessing a young child with hurt feelings—strikingly familiar. That's when I realized this was a learned behavior passed down through generations, something I was determined not to perpetuate with my own children.

It can be frowned upon when you choose to break cycles of bad behaviors. People may say you're acting differently because you are, and that's okay! Sometimes you outgrow the folks you've been brought up with. They can't handle your growth, and you have to know that's okay. I've learned that people who are meant to be in your life will be there, and those who were left behind might eventually come back around. You just might have been the one they had been watching who influenced their positive change.

In my early twenties, I realized that I needed to break away from what was familiar to me to start my growth journey. I moved to a city four hours from home, and making that move, both physically and emotionally, caused disruption. It wasn't easy, but five years later, I had worked my way up to a comfortable place in life, and I eventually met and later married my husband. This was the start of something special as we began building our lives together. This was also the start of my mother's disappointing, envious behavior.

I now had wife and mother responsibilities, and my mother seemed to resent that. Her behavior was aggressive at times when I attempted to have a healthy conversation about it. She began to intentionally cause friction and do things to purposely hurt me. When I put boundaries in place, it caused her to act out more and, of course, brought on that emotionally abusive roller coaster I was already familiar with. Contrary to how she always made me feel, I had to learn to be okay with knowing I'm not responsible for her feelings or her happiness. I realized that when we're frustrated or unable to think clearly, it can affect our ability to be who we need to be to our family.

My husband and I came from broken homes, so we knew we didn't want to repeat this cycle with our kids. We also realized that we couldn't continue to enable bad behavior from others, whether they are family or not. If you continue to enable bad behavior from a person, they will continue to display that bad behavior and will never be prompted to change. The manipulative actions of others in order to gain control are wrong, and you have to know that it's okay to opt out of allowing it.

Many people live with unresolved trauma, and I feel that if they would learn how to process their trauma healthily, their lives would improve. I choose to do better as an adult because I now know better. I choose to honor my mother by taking care of my health and ensuring that I don't treat my kids the way I was treated. I didn't want to continue this painful cycle and give my kids this pain to recover from. I believe that God gives us resources to help us, but it's up to us to properly manage and screen any of the resources or counsel we receive. I've learned to be very careful and pay attention to the reality of the person giving the advice or counsel. If someone has never gone through an experience, they can't genuinely share all that comes with it. And that's why I wrote this book—because I've been there. But more importantly, I got out of it.

Many attempt to bury their trauma, but it can show up in their way of living. Because they never learned to process their trauma, it can eventually take a toll on their health. You can only hide this pain for so long until it is exposed. You won't have to say a word because those who recognize what's happening will see it clearly.

The people in your life may be reaping the effects of the unresolved trauma you suffered, as I did from my mother. It's your job to stop that from happening. It won't be easy; unlearning and relearning were some of the hardest things I've ever done. I continue to do so every day, and you know what? It's worth it.

CHAPTER 2

"EVERYTHING IN ADULTHOOD CAN BE TRACED BACK TO CHILDHOOD" — PENNY JUNOR

There's a child in each of us, especially those who never had the ideal childhood. It may not feel like it, but that child is there in all your adult parts.

She's there in your choices and thoughts, the ones you make on autopilot that feel like second nature to you. She's there in your habits and mannerisms, in the practicalities of your life, in how you approach your job, in your relationship with friends, your husband, or your child. She's there, lurking, influencing, and directing because everything you are sprang from the child she once was.

She's there in all the little things you should know how to do but don't, like sharing or riding a bike. She's there in the adult who throws tantrums, the one who doesn't know how to have a relationship or never learned to love. Our adulthood was shaped by everything we were taught or not taught as children; childhood is the foundation of our lives. It's the place where we are taught to believe in dreams, love, or hope; it's also where we lose them.

King Solomon knew exactly what he was talking about when he said, "Start children off on the way they should go" (Proverbs 22:6, NIV). The wisdom with which he said it came directly from God. Many people mistake that Bible verse for one about training kids for chores and etiquette. And while that's part of it, it's only a minuscule part. It's not just about teaching your kids manners or having them make their bed every morning. It's also about teaching them how to love and dream and giving them the tools to live a purposeful life. This verse can serve as a reminder of why paying attention to Solomon's words is important, because broken children often turn into broken adults who raise even more broken children.

When you think of your childhood, what is the first thing that comes to mind? Do you think of it fondly? Nostalgically? Or have you blocked out painful memories from a time that should have been one of the happiest of your life? If your answer is the latter, then right now, you are the adult walking around with unresolved trauma. You are the adult making terrible life decisions because, as a child, you were never taught or shown how to make the right ones. Indeed, everything in adulthood can be traced to childhood. And if you think your current situation, your life, and your choices have nothing to do with your time as a child, then ask yourself this simple question: If your ten-year-old self could see you now, what would she think or say?

Many of us have gone through adverse childhood experiences.

Some of us are fully aware of our trauma but have no way to deal with it or have been told to ignore it; while some of us walk around completely unaware of the trauma we carry. When you were a child, your mind was fertile soil, and on it, the weeds or fruits of your existence were grown. It's why renewing your mind will not happen in a vacuum. It has to begin with unearthing everything you learned and believed as a child.

Have you ever heard of **adverse childhood experiences** (ACEs)? You likely have, but perhaps what you don't know is that your life is marked by some of them. How? Let's break down the meaning of adverse childhood experiences. After all, if you are clearing out a farm or garden, you have to know what's there so you can tackle it with the right tools.

What Are Adverse Childhood Experiences?

According to the Center for Disease Control, adverse childhood experiences (ACEs) are traumatic events that occur in a child's life between the age of zero and seventeen. They include:

- Experiencing violence, abuse, or neglect
- Witnessing violence in the home or community
- Having a family member attempt or die by suicide
- Living in an environment that's perpetually surrounded by death and violence
- Being abused by an authority or familial figure
- Living with or dealing with a suicidal family member or friend
- Losing a parent or loved one
- Emotional, sexual, or physical abuse
- Parental neglect
- Household challenges such as severe financial constraints, i.e., living in abject poverty
- Divorce
- Living with a family member who dealt with alcohol or substance abuse
- Incarceration of a family member
- Living with a mentally ill parent
- Witnessing any form of racial discrimination against a loved one or someone of a similar race

- Struggling with a medical issue, i.e., dealing with cancer at a young age
- Bullying
- Witnessing or being in the thick of a natural or manmade disaster
- Refugee or war experiences
- Spiritual or religious abuse

The list could go on and on. To simplify, think of an experience in your childhood that affected you so severely that it warped your view of yourself, people, the world, and even God. For instance, the sudden death of a parent or loved one might have you questioning God or the meaning of life.

Adverse childhood experiences are common—unbelievably common. According to the Substance Abuse and Mental Health Services Administration, in 2019, 1,840 children died of abuse and neglect in the United States.

We live in a fallen, broken world where bad things happen. Though originally made to be perfect, our world is imperfect, just like we are. So, even when we don't mean to hurt anyone or are innocent, it doesn't mean we will be spared from evil. If anything, bad things seek out good people; just look at Job. God never wanted a world where children had to deal with adverse experiences that broke them. And though it doesn't look or feel like that, God always has a remedy, even for the most broken people.

Is One Adverse Childhood Experience Worse Than Another?

When adults think of ACEs or trauma, they think of it in extremes, like a child experiencing death, suicide, or some form of neglect. You probably went through that previous list and thought, *Oh, none of that happened to me; I'm good.* But adverse childhood experiences aren't always so big or noticeably obvious. Sometimes they are little things done over time that compound into one big, traumatizing experience.

For instance, not being great at sports in an environment that glorifies it may have made you feel like you weren't good at anything or that the things you were great at weren't valuable enough. It would have you doubting your abilities or yearning to be someone you're not.

Conforming to a certain standard of beauty at a young age may have made you think you were not as beautiful as you are. For instance, many Black girls grew up thinking their natural hair was not good enough because they were forced to conform to a hairstyle created by a white standard.

Being talked over or shunned by parents, siblings, or friends as a child may have made you feel like your opinions weren't valuable or that your voice did not deserve to be heard. In time, it may have turned you into the adult who suffers social anxiety or nods with a fixed smile when everyone else contributes to a conversation.

Not being invited to parties thrown by classmates or other children your age as a child may have made you feel less accepted. Always being picked last at dodgeball may have made you feel a bit useless. Rejection by a crush or a terrible heartbreak may have scarred you and skewed your view of love and intimacy.

Being yelled at or hurried while eating your food may make you unable to share your food or relax and enjoy a meal. There are many more instances of childhood trauma; even when they aren't done with the intent to hurt, they still do. Even now, some adults still adopt the "children should be seen, not heard" style of rearing. But do you know what happens when you raise a child to believe they should not speak unless spoken to? You raise an adult incapable of standing up for themselves or others.

You might be thinking, *Okay, I went through that, and I'm fine*. But are you? Everyone processes trauma differently. Perhaps you and your siblings grew up in a similar abusive environment, and they appear put together, thriving even, so you are afraid or embarrassed to tell them that you can't make a friend. Or are you still afraid to let yourself get too close to anyone because your best friend moved away when you were ten?

Everyone deals with trauma differently; some families, even Christian families, don't deal with it at all. This leads us to another obvious but overlooked form of adverse childhood experience: invalidating trauma.

Experiencing trauma is one thing, but having it denied and overlooked can be just as traumatizing. And this is one thing many Christians are guilty of. There's a quote by John Hollingsworth that brings this to the forefront:

"So why do Christians have such a hard time letting each other express negative emotions?"

There are many Christians who cannot confront the truth of their trauma or help their children and loved ones confront theirs. This often happens because sometimes we Christians can tend to be miracle-centered, where we would take a miracle over putting in the work or acknowledging that traumas or negativity affect us the way they do unbelievers.

Some of us might think we are above trauma, that we are above pain, sorrow, sadness, or even depression. And when we find ourselves veering toward it, we might think that a quick pep talk or a graphic with a quote or Bible verse on a social media page will fix our feelings. Don't get me wrong, God's word is the most powerful thing in the world. But God also understands that there will come a moment when you are too broken to say the words. In those moments, your unadulterated expression of brokenness and pain to Him will be just as beautiful as any verse you quote or worship song you sing.

Another reason many Christians don't deal with their trauma is because they are afraid of being called crazy or faithless. It's like, "How can you believe in

God and be depressed? What do you mean you have unresolved trauma? Those things don't apply to children of God."

But remember when Lazarus died? And Jesus—knowing that He could raise Lazarus right there and then and that even if He didn't, Lazarus would rise again on the resurrection—still wept. He was moved by the sorrow of Martha and Mary, who had just lost their brother, so He wept. He didn't try to invalidate their sorrow; He didn't admonish them for mourning but instead wept with them. His weeping was so heartfelt that the Jews watching said, *...See how he loved him!* (John 11:36, NIV).

Jesus wept for His friend, yet a few minutes later, He was raising Lazarus from the dead. If God recognizes trauma, then who are you to deny yours when you desperately need healing?

An invalidated or neglected traumatic experience adds to the negative experience. When it happens to a child (or even an adult), it makes them feel unseen, unheard, or fearful that something is wrong with them. It also makes them distrust anyone who points their trauma out to them. Eventually, the child can grow into an adult who buries their feelings or trauma for fear they may be seen as weak or dramatic.

Does that sound like you?

Have you pushed down your trauma to the very depths of your soul, afraid that if you let yourself be vulnerable, you could get hurt? Has your trauma been invalidated so much that you don't think it's real anymore? You are afraid it's all in your head. It's not; it's never been, and the more you push down or ignore your trauma, the harder it becomes for you to truly heal.

Unresolved trauma hurts physically and spiritually. Scientific evidence shows how a person's health deteriorates due to unresolved trauma. Your inner child is hurting; she has spent so long being hurt, and it's your job as the adult to comfort her, ease her brokenness, and do for yourself what the adults in your life wouldn't do for you as a child.

Maybe misguided Christians are quoting scriptures to you, making you feel crazy for trying to fix yourself. Maybe all the graphics with Bible verses on social media don't do it for you anymore. Maybe you've been told to pray about it, and although you have, you still feel that ache in your soul.

Maybe you've prayed so much and you're now convinced that God doesn't care, because if He did, He wouldn't let you hurt like this.

Don't give up. The fact that you are reading this book right now means you are headed in the right direction. You see, one of the most unfortunate things about Christians who invalidate the negative experiences of others is that they often do it with scripture. This further perpetuates the false notion and misconception that God doesn't care about our trauma or how we feel. On the contrary, God cares deeply, and the Bible is filled with verses that support this. We will explore many of them in the chapters ahead.

If you still have doubts about what unresolved trauma can do to you or if you're unsure about its effects, please continue reading. There's a whole chapter dedicated to this topic that will shed a clear light on it.

CHAPTER 3

YOU ARE NOT FINE, NOT REALLY

How We Are Affected by Unresolved ACEs

There are three ways adverse childhood experiences can impact you as an adult: physically, psychologically, and spiritually. According to the Centers for Disease Control and Prevention, ACEs are linked to substance abuse in adults, chronic health problems, and mental illness. Science and modern medicine primarily focus on the physical and psychological aspects of ACEs. However, it's essential to remember that we are spiritual beings, and sometimes the physical manifestations of our experiences can be traced back to spiritual influences. The Bible has let us know that... *our struggle is not against flesh and blood, but against the rulers, against the authorities, against the powers of this dark world and against the spiritual forces of evil in the heavenly realms*

(Ephesians 6:12, NIV). So, to think our obstacles and issues are solely physical would be shortsighted.

The devil can exploit our physical weaknesses to attack us spiritually. For instance, the devil used Solomon's affection for foreign women to lead his heart away from God. He manipulated David's desire for Bathsheba, causing him to sin against God. The devil even attempted to exploit Jesus' obvious exhaustion and hunger from fasting for forty days to tempt Him into sinning against God. The devil is cunning and constantly seeks ways to draw you away from your spiritual path and God's calling on your life. However, here's the AMAZING thing: we ARE stronger than the devil. Through Jesus, God has granted us power over him. The devil cannot enter our hearts or manipulate us unless we allow him into our minds. If you've unintentionally allowed the devil to influence your life, renewing your mind has never been more crucial.

That said, let's go into the science and see just how much our unresolved ACEs affect us.

Physical Effects of ACEs in Adults

According to **Aces Aware**, a health initiative dedicated to screening adults for ACEs to help improve their lives, ACEs can be strongly associated with some of the most common, serious, and costly health conditions. ACEs are also often the primary cause of toxic stress, which arises from negative and repeatedly unresolved experiences that have been or are damaging to the individual. Adults who have endured ACEs are more susceptible to stress toxicity.

As we know, the world can be a stressful place—from leaving home in the morning to get to work, to having a long day at the office, to baking three dozen cupcakes for your son's class on short notice. However, stress can be beneficial. **Aces Aware** describes positive and tolerable stress as the beneficial kind.

Positive stress is the type you experience when participating in a sport, taking a test, or working to meet a deadline. It elevates your heart rate, which can be beneficial.

Tolerable stress is the type that occurs once. For instance, if as a child you witnessed the death of your grandmother but your mom helped you get through it in a healthy way, your brain adapts. So, instead of being traumatized by death, you see it as an inevitable passage for everyone who lives. And if you are a believer, you understand that for us, death is not the end.

Toxic stress, on the other hand, is the kind that accumulates in your body due to repeated abuse. Essentially, this type of stress builds up and can lead to trauma because the abuse was constant and there was no adult to help mitigate the effects. In fact, in most cases, the adult is the one causing stress to the child or another adult.

Regular stress signals your body's needs and serves as a reminder to take things slow or have a break. For instance, suppose you've been working long hours at the office or tirelessly without breaks. In that case, your body will eventually alert you that you need a break by causing burnout, leaving you with no choice but to rest.

However, toxic stress is persistent and pervasive stress resulting from ACEs or other traumatic experiences. For example, if you grew up in a home with an alcoholic, abusive, or neglectful parent, this kind of stress wasn't a one-week or few months' occurrence; it was constant. The more you experienced it, the harder it became for your body to resist or even signal you to fight it; it became your normal. This kind of stress lingers within you, infiltrates your bones, and makes it nearly impossible for you to naturally combat the stress. Essentially, your stress is constantly active, and it's this type of stress that leaves you vulnerable to various serious health conditions.

According to **Betterhelp**, the following illnesses are common in adults who experienced ACEs in their childhood: heart disease, liver disease, strokes, diabetes, and cancer. Toxic stress from ACEs can also lead to reduced immunity, obesity, asthma, and eczema. People have been known to make fun of obese individuals, assuming it's due to a lack of self-control or gluttony. They might say, "Well, maybe if you just ate healthier, you wouldn't be sick." But that's not always the case. While there are people who need to improve their eating habits, it's essential to withhold judgment when you encounter individuals struggling with obesity and diabetes because you may not know the challenges they've faced in childhood or throughout their lives.

There is also evidence suggesting that stress from ACEs can alter a person's genes. According to an article by a professor in the Department of Psychiatry, Neurology, Neuroscience, and The Institute of Genetic Medicine at Johns Hopkins University, this genetic change is profound and irreversible. When a child goes through a very traumatic experience, the body reacts by increasing the production of stress hormones and inflammation-related proteins, which then affect the child's DNA, essentially altering it. These altered DNA cells persist throughout life, making your body more susceptible to diseases and illnesses that your ancestors never had to deal with.

An adult with no family history of cancer may be suffering from cancer, all because they experienced ACEs as a child. Awful, isn't it?

Psychological Effects of ACEs on Adults

Research conducted in 2013 by the **National Library of Medicine** revealed that adults who have experienced ACEs are more likely to suffer from depression or borderline personality disorder. The younger and more vulnerable the child is, the more intense the effects will be in adulthood.

Additionally, adults who went through ACEs are at a higher risk of experiencing suicide, anxiety, or depression. According to **Betterhelp**, they are also more likely to develop PTSD.

Adults with ACEs tend to have poorer mental and psychological health, even if it's not as severe as depression or borderline personality disorder. They are more inclined to engage in self-destructive behaviors or, as **Betterhelp** notes, participate in risky physical and social activities. Some of these behaviors include extreme sports, sexual promiscuity, and reckless driving. Have you ever encountered someone who appeared determined to harm themselves, consistently making poor choices even when the right path was evident? Or perhaps they seemed to derive some twisted pleasure from hurting themselves or those around them. There's a high likelihood that such a person experienced ACEs.

Most adults who exhibit abusive or neglectful behavior were once children who experienced ACEs themselves. Consider parents or grandparents who survived civil wars, the Holocaust, were slaves or descendants of slaves, or lived during times of adverse racism. Similarly, reflect on parents who had strict, authoritarian, or abusive parents themselves. These adults may have become toxic because they lacked the support needed to address their own traumas; there was no adult figure to mitigate the effects of their experiences. Consequently, without an alternative model, they embraced the only way they knew, often perpetuating the cycle of trauma, which subsequently affected their children.

Adults who have experienced ACEs are also more likely to encounter employment-related issues. In some cases, they may lack the motivation to excel in any particular endeavor, while in others, they may struggle to maintain steady employment. Occasionally, you may encounter an adult who possesses significant potential but appears oblivious to it or lacks the intention to harness it. Perhaps they have endured a lifetime of being labeled as worthless, leading them to overlook their distinctive talents and abilities.

Adults who have experienced ACEs are also at a higher risk of displaying sexual, physical, or emotional aggression toward others in their lives. For example, some parents believe that the only way to discipline a child is through physical punishment because they were disciplined this way as children. Others may think that withholding praise is the only way to motivate a child. This may seem twisted, and indeed it is. In reality, under the right circumstances, encouragement can inspire positive actions. Were you the child who came home, proud of achieving a high test score or earning a spot in the school play, only to have your parents downplay your accomplishment, acting as if it was no big deal? Do you find yourself unconsciously replicating this behavior with your own child?

Some people believe that withholding praise from their children will make them better individuals, while offering praise will make them arrogant. There are parents who react to simple childhood mistakes by screaming at or cursing their children. Some parents struggle with effective communication and listening when it comes to their children.

Also, there are men who cheat on and abuse their wives because they witnessed their fathers doing the same to their mothers. Similarly, there are women who endure abusive marriages because they saw their mothers doing so. Children learn primarily through observation, and no matter what you tell a child, if your actions don't align with your words, they will not follow your guidance. It's possible that your own parents experienced trauma that they didn't recognize as such, and they inadvertently perpetuated the cycle by passing it on to you. The saying goes, "Hurt people hurt people," and this cycle will persist until someone takes the initiative to step out of it and break it.

Spiritual Effects: How the Devil Uses Our Trauma Against Us

Traumas often manifest in physical ways. It could be the mother who physically abuses you at the slightest provocation or for no reason at all, or the father who becomes abusive when he's drunk. Perhaps you live in an environment marked by violence and death, where gunshots are a regular occurrence, so much so that you no longer react to the sound. These events are physical and tangible, and the pain and heartbreak they bring are equally real. However, it's important to understand that even though our traumas and their effects may appear physical, they can also have a spiritual dimension. As Ephesians 12:6 tells us, our struggle is not merely against physical forces. In reality, things often run much deeper because the devil is known to work tirelessly behind the scenes. The Bible says he comes *to steal and kill and destroy* (John 10:10, NIV). But it's a good thing that God works harder, because that same verse reminds us that Jesus came so that we may have life and have it abundantly.

The devil often uses those closest to us to steal, kill, and destroy. It's crucial to understand that anything not rooted in love does not come from God; it originates from the devil, and it should be recognized as such. Not everyone operates in the light of God, especially those who inflict harm and abuse on others, even if they happen to be friends or family members. But God provides us with ways to address such situations. Stay tuned, as we will delve into these strategies in the upcoming chapters. For now, let's focus on how the devil attempts to exploit our wounds, including those we inflict on others, to harm us.

When someone who is supposed to protect, love, or remain loyal to you ends up hurting you, the sense of betrayal and pain can be overwhelming. It's hard to believe that the person you trusted would do such a thing, and it's natural for these emotions to fuel your hatred and anger toward them. You may find yourself carrying these feelings with you wherever you go, nurturing them, thinking that by doing so, you are getting back at or hurting the person who harmed you. However, this couldn't be further from the truth.

In many cases, those who have hurt you may never realize the extent of the damage they've caused, and even if they do, they may never take responsibility or offer an apology. Consider the Egyptians and their treatment of the Israelites as an example; they enslaved them and subjected them to unimaginable suffering, even killing their babies. Yet, there is no part of the Bible that indicates they apologized or acknowledged the wrong they committed. Instead, even after being forced to release the Israelites through God's intervention, the Egyptians still attempted to pursue them.

By holding onto hurt, anger, or resentment, you end up hurting only yourself, and in doing so, you allow the devil to win. The devil thrives on using our past against us, whether it's a past where we've hurt someone or where someone has hurt us. He has a way of making you feel like a victim, convincing you that you could never possibly recover from what's been done to you or what you've done to others.

The devil wants you to dwell in your trauma, to blame it on your mother's narcissism or your father's neglect. He wants you to use it as a justification for every risky behavior or bad decision you make. He wants you to keep saying, "I don't know how to love because nobody ever loved me." But these are all lies. You may be broken and damaged, but there is nothing so damaged that God can't mend, and no sin so terrible that He cannot forgive.

By keeping you focused on reliving your past, the devil is attempting to prevent you from embracing your future, which he knows is filled with greatness. He wants to trap you in that place where your mother or father abused you or in the trauma that once sought to shatter you. Instead of letting go and taking responsibility for your choices as an adult, he wants you to continue blaming everyone for what occurred during your childhood. God knows how harmful our toxic past can be to us. It's why He says, *Get rid of all bitterness, rage and anger, brawling and slander, along with every form of malice* (Ephesians 4:31, NIV). It's also why He says, *Forget the former things; do not dwell on the past. See, I am doing a new thing!* (Isaiah 43:18-19, NIV). But unfortunately, rather than turning to this verse and embracing the promise of it, the devil tries to keep us stuck in our painful memories.

Our memories are a significant part of who we are; they can shape, drive, or burden us. Perhaps, when you think of your mother or father, you only remember how they hurt you, how they abandoned you, how they beat you, and those nights when you felt sure you would not survive their abuse. The devil keeps these painful memories at the forefront and obscures the fact that, yes, you endured severe trauma, but God preserved your life for a purpose.

In some instances, the devil may make you believe that what happened to you was your fault. He will keep you trapped in that memory where you thought maybe people would love you if you weren't so worthless. He might tell you it was your fault you got raped, your father abandoned you because you weren't good enough, or your mother beat you because you were evil. Our minds are our most potent weapons, which is why the devil loves to manipulate them. Why? Because once he has you believing lies about yourself and your identity, he can rob you of everything God has planned for you. The physical and psychological effects of ACEs are challenging enough without allowing the devil to manipulate you spiritually. Your spiritual life is a crucial aspect, and that's why the devil loves to meddle with it, knowing that if he keeps you stuck there, he can hinder every other aspect of your life.

You Need to Stop Sinking Your Boat

Allowing the devil to make you hold on to pain, hurt, resentment, anger, or any other grudges is like sinking your own boat. Let me elaborate with a story:

A man was on a boat, and it was sinking. He called the Coast Guard for help. The Coast Guard hurried to come, but the man was too far away and they couldn't reach him quickly enough. So they asked the man:

"Hey, do you have any load on the boat?"

"Yes," the man answered.

"What is it?" the Coast Guard asked.

"Water. I took on gallons of water from the sea."

"How many?"

"It covers half the boat," the man said proudly.

The man from the Coast Guard shook his head in surprise and said, "There's nothing special about that water. You don't need it. It's salty. The weight is sinking your boat. Throw the water overboard so your boat can steady."

"No," the man replied, "I need it. I can't throw it overboard."

The man from the Coast Guard was perplexed. "Why not? It's just salty water. We have cleaner, fresher water on the shore. If you throw that water over, you can have as much as you want when you come ashore."

"No!" the man insisted. "I can't throw it overboard. I've been carrying this water around. I'm not just going to throw it away. I need it."

The Coast Guard officer tried convincing the man, but he wouldn't throw the water overboard. Finally, the officer said to the man:

"You have a choice to make: throw the water overboard and keep your boat afloat. Or leave the water in your boat and sink with it."

Isn't it ridiculous that the man must think about this? His life is at stake. Still, he hangs on to gallons of water he doesn't need.

That's how it looks when you carry all that hurt, pain, anger, and resentment. It might seem like you need it, but you don't. And the sooner you throw the water overboard, the sooner you can row your boat to safety and fresh, clean water.

CHAPTER 4

DO YOU BELIEVE THE THOUGHT MAKES THE PERSON?

Most people don't examine what they think about, which is alarming because our minds are swirling with thoughts every single minute of every single day. So, to go through life completely unaware of what you are thinking and how those thoughts are shaping your life is frightening.

I believe that thoughts make the person. But I would not have known this if I had not become aware of the limiting beliefs and thoughts that were restricting my life.

The thing about limiting beliefs is that they appear so true, so normal, so acceptable…sometimes not just to you, but to everyone around you. They feel like gospel truth, especially because they have become so ingrained in your mind that the thought of believing anything else seems ludicrous. That's how powerful limiting beliefs are—powerful enough that they have you living a life and following a pattern that's not yours.

Lifehack defines limiting beliefs as a state of mind, conviction, or belief that you feel to be true and that limits you in some way.

I think of limiting beliefs as lies about yourself, others, or your circumstances that you believe to be true. They may seem like absolute truths, but they are lies. Limiting beliefs are tricky because they present themselves as realistic assertions about who you are or what you are capable of. Right now, you probably don't think of your limiting beliefs as negative thoughts; you most likely think of them as realistic.

For instance, as a parent, you might think that pursuing your career dreams to whatever height you want to attain is not only unrealistic but also selfish. This thought could stem from your belief that, as a parent, your whole life should revolve around your children.

As a woman, you might think you need to be ruthless to attain a position generally held by a man, and if you're *not* ruthless, there's no way you can ever achieve this goal.

As a Christian, you may believe that being poor is who or what you are supposed to be, because being rich would keep you away from God. Many Christians believe it is righteous to be poor. Let me assure you that it's not.

As a forty-year-old, you may think you are too old to start again or change your life. Or as a forty-year-old woman, you might believe you are too old to get a husband.

As a minority man or woman, you might think your race will prevent you from fully attaining your potential. You might shy away from taking on certain positions or applying for them because you think you have to be white to get them.

Every day, people walk around with limiting thoughts. There are millions of people living and breathing like that. It's awful when you think about it, that these people have allowed lies to become the foundation of their existence. If you walked up to a random person and asked them to list some positive things about themselves (unless you met a truly confident or self-assured person), it might take them a while to answer. Most people are used to thinking of themselves in a dim light, and if you turned on a light on how amazing they are, they wouldn't know how to accept it.

Limiting beliefs make us create lies about ourselves and situations that don't align with what God has said about us. More importantly, limiting beliefs stem from our unbelief in God's direction in our lives or the sufficiency that He provides. 2 Timothy 1:7, NIV says, "For the Spirit God gave us does not make us timid, but gives us power, love, and self-discipline." If we understand this, then we must understand that limiting beliefs have no place in our hearts.

Limiting beliefs are the lies we pick up in our journey through life. Unfortunately, as humans, we have a tendency to fixate on the negative rather than the positive. But have you ever really paid attention to the actions of a little baby? They can be so bold and daring. They can be unstoppable, especially when they start to walk or crawl. They don't believe that their abilities are restricted or that there's a world out there to hurt them. Every time they fall, they get back up. But as they grow up, as they mature, they start to encounter experiences and actions that make them form limiting beliefs. They feel they are not smart enough, strong enough, or talented enough.

Every limiting belief you hold was learned or imitated. You were not created to think of yourself as not good enough or not smart enough; you were taught all of that.

Sources of Limiting Beliefs

Family Values and Beliefs

For children, family is their first image of what society should be or look like. That's why family is called the smallest unit of society. It's within this facet that children learn and grow, and it's from there they are taught to chase or pursue their dreams or to give them up.

Sometimes the limiting beliefs acquired from family come in the form of abuse. Perhaps your father or mother repeatedly told you or made you feel you were not good enough. Abuse plays a major role in shaping a child's beliefs about themselves and the people they come in contact with. If a father beats his daughter viciously and repeatedly and then tells her he does it because he loves her, she can grow up expecting that her husband or boyfriend should beat her. And if he doesn't, she could conclude it's because he doesn't love her. She could have formed this toxic, limiting belief about herself that there's something inherently wrong with her, something that deserves to be beaten.

On the other hand, limiting beliefs don't always stem from emotional or physical abuse. Ironically, they can originate from parents trying to shield their children from disappointment and hurt. For instance, imagine a child who grew up aspiring to be an astronaut, but their parents encourage them to pursue something more practical because they don't believe the child has what it takes to become an astronaut and want to spare them heartbreak.

Similarly, witnessing parents in a loveless marriage might lead a child to believe that love within a marriage is unattainable, or if it is, it's not meant for someone like them. Maybe you're an adult who finds it challenging to speak up against unjust authority because your parents instilled in you the belief that authority should never be challenged. If a child is scolded for expressing their thoughts when they're trying to communicate, it might lead them to believe they should never speak their mind.

Consider a child who falls while playing, and the mother overreacts. This could lead the child to believe they are fragile. If a child experiences failure in a competition or any endeavor, and their parents discourage them from trying again (perhaps to shield them from disappointment), it might instill a fear of taking chances and a belief that they would inevitably fail if they tried.

Parents have a knack for instilling beliefs about their children, whether through words or actions. The child, in turn, often accepts these beliefs as truths and begins to live in accordance with them. As a parent, it's crucial to understand that being overly protective of your children can inadvertently limit their potential.

Limiting beliefs that originate within families often revolve around prescribed roles that you're expected to conform to. For example, if you were born into a family with strict gender roles that rigidly define the responsibilities of men and women, you might grow up believing that a woman should not pursue a career or anything beyond being a wife and mother.

There are also limiting beliefs that are unrelated to gender but are meant to keep you within the confines of a particular mold. For instance, if your father spent his entire life working as a mechanic in his small auto-shop, he might expect you to follow the same path. He might perceive your desire to pursue something different as a lack of respect for his work or a failure to be proud of him. You might even agree with these sentiments because you've witnessed your father always approaching his work with a chip on his shoulder. Subconsciously, you may feel compelled to maintain that same attitude.

Limiting beliefs stemming from family can be exceptionally challenging to overcome. It becomes difficult to envision yourself as someone different, someone who can break free from the mold your family has established, especially when you lack examples to emulate. It's almost like going against your very essence.

Do you relate to that? Have you attempted to transform your life, to shift your beliefs, only to be reminded by your father, mother, or another family member—either through their words or actions—that you are who you are, and there's no altering that? In familial contexts, we often hold onto the notion that the apple doesn't fall far from the tree. Yet, we tend to forget about the harvester, the one who gathers the apples, fallen or not, to craft something new and exciting. So, if your father was an apple pie, who dictates that you must be a pie as well? While it's true that the apple doesn't stray too far from the tree, each apple can be transformed into something distinct. The only way you're destined to replicate your parents' mistakes, the sole means by which you remain ensnared by limiting beliefs, is if you don't consciously steer the course you wish to follow.

Environment and Society

Many of the choices we make are influenced by what we observe and how we interact with our environment. Our current environment is one where everyone is striving to be an influencer. Often, without realizing it, we adopt and internalize beliefs about ourselves from random posts on social media, even when these beliefs have nothing to do with our true selves. The people you choose to follow on social media shape your perception of ideas and self-worth, reflecting a part of your own identity. For instance, if you follow a content creator who frequently shares self-deprecating humor about themselves, it's not merely because you find it amusing. It could be because, deep down, you believe you share a connection with them, a form of kinship.

Every day, we engage with events and actions that shape our beliefs. For example, consider a minority child who has grown up in an environment tainted by racism. Even in situations where there is no evident bias or danger, they may still perceive it due to the influence of society and their personal experiences. If you reside in a society where the wealthy seem to escape consequences for their actions, you might develop the belief that justice is elusive for the less privileged.

Our surroundings serve as teachers, influencing us even when we are not actively engaged in learning. This is why God reminds us through His word that we are not of this world; we must remain distinct from it, or else everything God calls us to believe may seem like a falsehood. Your immediate environment may have burdened you with limiting beliefs that constrain your potential. The reassuring truth is that God operates in an environment filled with boundless possibilities.

Our Experiences

Ever heard the term "fool me once"? Of course you have. It implies that if you're fooled once, it's your own fault if it happens again. Many people who grew up in relatively good environments with strong family values still harbor limiting beliefs that originated from negative experiences. Let's say you gave your all in a romantic relationship and had your heart broken in a public and painful manner. This could lead to one of two reactions: you might proceed cautiously in future relationships, or you might conclude that love inevitably leads to heartbreak.

Alternatively, perhaps you've been working diligently for a promotion that you ultimately don't receive. This could lead to the belief that hard work doesn't pay off, or you didn't get the promotion because you simply weren't good enough. Being ridiculed for attempting something new might make you doubt your abilities and deter you from trying again. Repeated failures might lead you to believe that you're not intelligent.

Limiting beliefs take root and thrive in our minds because we often fail to recognize that the negative emotions stemming from these experiences are temporary. It's entirely normal to feel sadness or heartbreak when things don't go as planned. However, what's not okay is allowing one moment of disappointment to define your entire life.

When you encounter a challenging experience, rather than viewing it as the ultimate verdict on the course of your life, consider it a valuable lesson or a character-building challenge. Your limiting beliefs should not be equated with what God believes about you. In His eyes, you are wonderfully made. After all, He is the Creator who designed you.

Effects of Limiting Childhood Beliefs in Our Adult Lives

The most harmful aspect of limiting beliefs is their acceptance and normalcy. They can turn you into someone who is complacent with the status quo, content to remain in the shadows, and comfortable with being comfortable. It's this comfort in limiting beliefs that perpetuates their persistence. A new generation observes the mediocrity of the old generation and may think, *Well, they didn't achieve anything great with their lives, but they seem okay.* This normalization of something so toxic is detrimental, and it goes against God's plan for our lives.

Limiting beliefs make you complicit in the destruction of your life. Every time you say, "I can't," the devil is right there ensuring that you won't. Limiting beliefs rob you of a good and fulfilling life, which is precisely the life God intends for you. They turn you into a liar, and in turn, you make God out to be a liar. Why? Because God did not lie when He said you were wonderfully made. Even if that wonder doesn't manifest in your physical appearance, it's evident in all the unique qualities and paths God designed for you. Why do you think the devil is so invested in derailing your life? Because he knows your beliefs about yourself are lies, and he doesn't want you to discover the truth. Limiting beliefs don't just harm you; they can also impact the people around you. They have the potential to infect your children and those who look up to you. Our perception and beliefs about who we are and what we can do have a ripple effect on everyone in our lives. By rejecting your own gifts and potential, you may inadvertently encourage others to do the same. You might not realize it, but God could connect someone's success and growth to your beliefs. When you believe that you can do anything, it can inspire others to follow their own dreams.

Limiting beliefs prevent you from being your authentic self, and it's truly disheartening to go through life without knowing your true self due to the acceptance and internalization of false truths about yourself. Not only do these beliefs hinder you from embracing your true self, but they also cut off opportunities and blessings that are meant to come your way. It's akin to a woman convincing herself that she can't be a good mother and deciding not to become one. Perhaps God had chosen her for that role because He created her to be an exemplary mother. Imagine her leaving this world without fulfilling that purpose, and imagine the potential impact the child she was meant to raise could have had on the world.

These beliefs are not your fault. They've rooted themselves in your mind through life experiences and upbringing by parents who may not have known how to raise a child. I recognize that you've witnessed discouraging and overwhelming aspects of society. I know that, as a result, the person you truly want to be might seem like a fantasy, an ideal version of yourself that could never exist.

I want you to set aside everything you've seen, heard, and believed and take a moment to ask yourself this question: "What does God believe about me?"

CHAPTER 5

YOUR GRANDMA'S FINE CHINA IS NOT THE ONLY THING YOU INHERITED

What is something your family does that's always been done that way? You can't trace its origins; it's just been a constant presence. Is it a negative influence, like an anchor holding you back? Or a positive one, like a sail propelling your ship forward? That enduring element woven into the very fabric of your family is referred to as a **generational pattern.**

Generational patterns consist of traits and habits that are passed down from generation to generation, whether intentionally or not. They can be minor things, like having chicken for dinner every Sunday, or more unfortunate things, like struggles with alcoholism. Before you convince yourself that you're exempt from generational patterns, let me reassure you that every family has them. Your grandmother's fine china isn't the only thing you've inherited.

Some generational patterns are positive; they serve as the building blocks that construct and sustain entire generations. These positive patterns encompass traits such as perseverance, patience, kindness, compassion, forgiveness, love, security, open communication, entrepreneurship, strength, and a sense of belonging, among others.

For instance, you might exhibit resilience because throughout your life, you've witnessed and heard that "the Johnsons never give up." Consequently, rather than dwelling on problems or complaints, you tend to adopt a solution-oriented approach. Alternatively, your attentive motherhood could stem from your own mother always being there to listen when you needed her, just as her mother was for her. Your devotion as a husband may have been instilled by your father's actions, which were passed down from his own father. Generational patterns can be beneficial in imparting values and morals that pave the way for a fulfilling life.

I believe that generational patterns are a part of God's original design. He created families with the purpose of nurturing and passing down positive qualities to their descendants. However, something happened between Adam and Cain that disrupted this design. As you can already see, generational patterns aren't always positive, and the negative ones tend to stand out.

Some people are too comfortable with being comfortable. Generational patterns can contribute to this. Potentials and talents can go to waste because a family has raised generations of quitters, people who are content with not making an effort. Maybe you come from a family where reaching a managerial position at Walmart is considered the ultimate achievement.

To be clear, there's nothing wrong with aspiring to be a Walmart manager. Humility, hard work, and honest labor will always be more valuable than purposeless ambition and an insatiable pursuit of wealth. Some people are genuinely meant to be Walmart managers, and while it may sound unconventional, it's true. Perhaps they were created to be kind and understanding managers for working moms and dads who are striving to pay their children's tuition, possibly for the next Supreme Court justice. In this scenario, they wouldn't be living a life of mediocrity; they would be precisely where God intended them to be.

Whether you're a maid or a manager, carry out your work with kindness and honesty, as there's a divine reason for your placement. Notice that I said God placed you, not that you settled there. There's a significant distinction. Don't settle for mediocrity when God has designated you for exceptional greatness.

The thing about generational patterns is that you may not recognize or acknowledge them until you step back and examine them. They are often glaring, just not to you. Some family patterns promote codependency, gambling, overworking, overeating, physical violence, promiscuity, lying, cheating, adultery, abuse, coasting, narcissism, poor money management, remarrying, and the like.

You can inherit generational patterns, whether you want to or not, whether you are aware of it or not. Observing your parents repeatedly engaging in certain behaviors, especially when they appear normal, may lead you to mimic those behaviors, whether you like them or not, particularly if you are not consciously working to avoid them. Generational patterns persist because people tend to parent the way they were parented.

Have you ever had someone say to you, "You are just like your mother"? For some adults, this is the worst thing you could say to them. For others, it's a beautiful compliment. Those in the first group may resent their parents, only to be told they are just like them. How could this be? How could they become the very thing they've spent their entire lives hating and trying to avoid? Generational patterns are tricky. The way to avoid them is not by acting as if you are above them (pride comes before a fall). It's by recognizing their existence and understanding that, unless you are intentional, you could easily become what you despise.

Understanding that you are not and don't have to be like your parents is the foundation of this book. The moment I grasped that concept, my life changed, and I can tell you firsthand that I am not the mother my own mother was. You can be just as different. But first, let's thoroughly explore generational patterns.

Hidden Generational Patterns and How They Affect Us

Hidden generational patterns encompass traits, characteristics, lifestyles, behaviors, and beliefs that are passed down from generation to generation. Ironically, these patterns are often glaringly obvious to everyone within a family except for the individuals themselves. I refer to them as hidden because, despite being plainly visible to those around, they are the very things that family members tend not to acknowledge. Moreover, there always seems to be a logical excuse or explanation for these patterns, such as someone saying, "Do you think my drinking is bad? My father used to beat me when he got drunk. I'm nothing like him! At least I don't hurt anyone!" We frequently employ these explanations as platitudes to soothe ourselves.

The Bible is replete with somewhat hidden generational patterns that have led to grave consequences. Let's examine two of them:

King David and His Sons (2 Samuel 11, 12, 13, & 14, NIV) (1 Kings 11 & 12, NIV)

David was an exceptional man and an even greater king. He was God's chosen king for the people of Israel, but he battled with lust. He did not need all of the wives he married or the concubines he took to his bed, but he had them nonetheless. And he certainly did not need to take another man's wife, but he did. We don't know how David's father, Jesse, fared with women or lust, but we can tell you that David's own children followed expressly in his footsteps. When you think about David's punishment in retrospect (the one God gave him for sleeping with Bathsheba and arranging for her husband's death), it was the pattern he created that almost led to the destruction of his lineage and the eventual division of Israel. However, God, ever faithful to His promises, kept His word to David, even though David was undeserving of it.

Now, let's examine the consequences of the pattern David created. He may be the most renowned king in the Old Testament, but he made some serious missteps.

David was so consumed by lust that he took Bathsheba for himself. He ordered his guards to bring her to him, and it's likely that she had little say in the matter. When she became pregnant, in an attempt to hide his sin and avoid the consequences of Bathsheba's husband discovering the adultery, David arranged for her husband to be killed. In turn, David's son Amnon was also driven by lust to the point where he forced himself upon his sister Tamar, raping her. Shockingly, David never punished Amnon for what he did to his sister. Absalom, Tamar's brother and Amnon's stepbrother, took matters into his own hands and murdered Amnon.

Both Amnon and Absalom followed David's pattern of entitlement, lust, and murder. Absalom felt entitled to seek revenge, leading to his murder of Amnon. Amnon, driven by lust and entitlement, committed the heinous act of raping his sister, mirroring David's sense of entitlement when he took Bathsheba for himself.

Many scholars assert that David did, in fact, rape Bathsheba. He ordered her to be brought to him and engaged in sexual relations with her. Bathsheba was fully aware of the dire consequences of adultery, as outlined in Leviticus 20:10-12. She knew that both she and her lover could face execution if their act was discovered. This knowledge weighed heavily on her, especially considering her husband's high rank in David's army and his involvement in a war for King David. But how could she refuse the advances of the most powerful king Israel had ever known?

Solomon displayed a similar level of lust. While the Bible does not record him raping any women, he accumulated a vast number of wives and concubines, enough to populate a small town. He continued to acquire women until he had a staggering one thousand to his name. This excessive desire for women is textbook lust in every sense. Solomon's insatiable lust led him away from God and resulted in him raising sons who neither knew nor followed the Lord. Eventually, Solomon drifted so far from God that he imposed forced labor on the people of Israel and their neighboring communities. When his son Rehoboam ascended to power, he promised to intensify Solomon's forced labor policies. Unsurprisingly, this led to the division of the country as the Israelites vehemently opposed such oppression. That's where the famous line "to your tents, Israel!" (1 Kings 12:16, NIV) comes from.

Imagine a whole nation being divided because of sons who copied their fathers, who copied *their* fathers. The consequences of our actions don't just affect us; they affect people around us, people we may never even meet.

Do you think David sat any of his sons down and told them to rape women or commit murders? No. Do you think they were in support of what he did with Bathsheba? Probably not. After all, having another wife meant more children, which meant less inheritance for the existing children. But they watched their father, and subconsciously or not, they copied him. David could retrace his steps and find his way back to God. But his sons, not so much. That's another thing about generational patterns; the effect differs for everyone.

Rebecca and Jacob (Genesis 25, 27, 30, and 37)

Rebecca had twin sons, and she quickly picked a favorite, Jacob. She loved him far more than her eldest son and desired him to receive his father's blessings ahead of his brother Esau, even though these blessings rightfully belonged to Esau by law and culture. Rebecca didn't let that deter her; she aided Jacob in deceiving her blind husband, Isaac. She helped him prepare the food that Isaac had requested from Esau before granting his blessings. She went to great lengths, dressing Jacob in hairy goatskin and Esau's clothes, so that the blind Isaac would mistake Jacob for Esau. When Esau discovered what his mother had done, he was heartbroken and filled with vengeance, even contemplating killing his brother. Do you notice the patterns here?

Jacob observed and learned much from his mother. He likely began to develop a sense of entitlement due to his mother's favoritism over his older brother.

Jacob would go on to become just as much of a trickster as his mother. He cheated his father-in-law, Laban (although Laban was no saint), cleverly breeding stronger animals for himself while keeping the weaker ones for Laban. Furthermore, he, like his mother, picked a favorite among his twelve sons: Joseph. This choice ignited hidden outrage and jealousy, ultimately leading to Joseph being nearly killed and eventually sold by his elder brothers, who were meant to protect him.

Do you think Rebecca sat Jacob down and said, "Listen, when you have twelve sons, make sure to pick a favorite. Ensure that you treat all of them differently, and be obvious about it"? The Bible says none of that, but consciously or not, Jacob was observing and learning.

These patterns might not be explicitly spelled out, but they are present. Frequently, the consequences of our actions are not the result of karma or divine punishment but are influenced by family patterns that we have unwittingly adopted.

That's why I opened with a question: What is something you do that's always been done in your family? Familial patterns are not always obvious to us. What we see as normal, even mundane, might cause a gasp of shock from another family. It might seem normal to you that all the women in your family end up divorced, but someone coming from a loving and devoted family may look at you in disbelief. It may seem normal to you that no one in your family has ever gone to college, perhaps because they see college as a complete waste of time and money, but someone else from a college-centered family may balk at this type of mindset.

It may seem normal to you that your father is a workaholic who was never home, even on holidays; you might even think that you turned out all right because of it. But someone whose father was always there might feel sorry for you. You are not fine if you find yourself not wanting to have kids because you think having a job would prevent you from being there for them. Or your father's workaholic attitude may lead you to become an obsessive overachiever.

Perhaps your mother put her life on hold to do a thankless job so she could take care of her parents. Never saving up, never living the life she deserved, never doing what she was made to do. And you do the same because you've been taught that it's called "honoring your parents." But someone else would look at you and label it as the term that originated in South Africa, "black tax": a form of income or a huge financial responsibility that often young Black professionals give to their family in a way that prevents them (the working professional) from taking care of themselves, living up to their full potential, or building generational wealth for their upcoming families.

The signs of generational patterns are always there. They're there in ACEs, in your uncontrollable anger, in how intrusive you are to your kids, or how dismissive you are of their feelings. They are there in how comfortable you are, in the fact that you won't shoot past mediocrity. They are there in your broken marriages, or the fact that you can't seem to keep a job. Or perhaps in how flaky or flippant you are. They are there in your insecurities or the negative beliefs you hold about yourself. They may seem hidden, but only to you, because they are so glaring to everyone else.

Generational patterns may seem impossible to break. In fact, the devil designed them in such a way that you would think they are impossible to break. So you might be thinking, *If my mother, and her mother, and her mother before her couldn't stay in their marriages, how am I supposed to? If my grandfather and his father couldn't let go of the bottle, how am I supposed to?*

Well, there's something called a cycle breaker, and hopefully, by the end of this book and with God's grace, that's what you'll become.

CHAPTER 6

IT'S NOT ALWAYS TRAUMA

This book is primarily about our ACEs and resulting trauma, and while they are very real and damaging, I would be doing you a huge disservice if I didn't touch on the fact that not all our limitations are caused by trauma. Some of us choose to blame our choices, decisions, and lifestyle on trauma that doesn't exist. It's easy to blame trauma or ACEs for all of our misfortunes. It's especially easy when you know deep down that the only one you have to blame is yourself.

There are too many people who are not living their purpose. Too many people who are just too comfortable with being comfortable. Too many people who don't understand that God did not put us on this earth to be comfortable or mediocre. He put us here to work, to establish, create, and inspire. Every time, for one reason or another, you choose to ignore the gift God has given you—every time you wake up and push it farther back on the shelf—you are not only denying yourself the wonder of your gift, but you are also denying the people God wants you to bless with it. Let's back up a little.

Most people are unable to achieve their purpose or reach their full potential because of one trauma or another. Those people have an excuse, and perhaps no one would blame them if they chose to sit in the corner and do nothing all day. In fact, people who have suffered horrific traumas or who are from a certain demographic, place, or gender are naturally not expected to excel or be more than what society thinks they should be. These people are expected to be poor, average, unintelligent, and unambitious. They are expected to be impoverished. They are expected to be the ones who take, who receive but never give.

But what about you?

Perhaps you grew up in an average family. Your mom was always there for you when you needed her. She packed your lunch, gave you kisses when you left and returned from school, allowed you to have friends over and fun sleepovers, and she scolded you when the need arose. She was not the perfect mom, but she loved you fiercely, and even when you were upset with her, you knew with all of your heart she would do anything for you.

Perhaps you had a dad who was always there. He protected you and defended you. Together, he and your mom made sure you always had the basics and then some. Sure, you could never go to Hawaii for vacation, but you almost always got the present you wanted for Christmas. Up until this time, you've had a good life, and good parents; you've never been exposed to anything too traumatizing, or at least not so traumatizing that you couldn't get over it eventually.

Some people with a childhood like that develop a certain comfort, a certain average mindset, a certain roadmap that is, in fact, in contrast with what God has given to them. They never faced challenges or real obstacles, and because of that, they don't understand what it means to push forward or yearn for something more. They are quite comfortable just being, never doing, never wanting to step out of the box to explore or create. Ironically, while your childhood may have been safe and comfortable, it may have also led you to believe that you are beneath or above some things. Or that maybe you are not the kind of person who owns and creates. Perhaps your childhood has made you believe that you are the kind of person who is meant to be an employee, never an employer. But surely, you hear that soft whisper in your heart, that gentle voice stirring you toward the more that you could be.

So, what's your excuse for not trying?

What's your excuse for not earnestly searching out and living your purpose? Trauma prevents us, attacks us, and tries to limit us, but what if in your case, the only person limiting you is you? What if all you need to do is step away from that place or thing that makes you too comfortable? This is not a judgment on you or on the way you were raised. This is a wake-up call. YOU need to stop being comfortable. There are people who will settle in everything: in love, in marriage, in career, in friendships and relationships; taking the crumbs handed to them, never trying to bake their own bread. But ask yourself, does that person have to be you?

I know, we live in a society that, against all odds, wants to keep the status quo—a society that aims to make certain things more attainable for some people than others. Perhaps you are in a circle of people who don't believe in trying, or perhaps you are wrapped up in a codependent relationship, one that amplifies your insecurities or has made you think you couldn't possibly survive on your own. Or perhaps you are just too comfortable with being comfortable. You need to shake that. There is nothing more damaging than a person stuck in a box, too afraid to step outside their comfort zone. It is actually the last thing God wants for you. You need to get up and move.

You see, the thing about life is we have choices. We are all born with free will, and although there are people who try to suppress that in one way or another, free will is always available through God. It's why your relationship with Him is so important. You have a choice to step away from the life you are living right now to the one God wants you to live. You need to allow yourself to be open to the world, to opportunities, to God's voice, and bury the thought that some things are just not attainable for people like you. The only thing you can't get is that which God prevents you from getting. Every other thing, by the grace of God, is perfectly within your reach.

Get up and get moving. Choose to do better and be better. You shouldn't let the voices of others or your "comfort" stop you from being who God has called you to be. God has made a path for each of us to walk through, but many of us are just too afraid to do the work. The Bible says, *If you are willing and obedient, you will eat the good things of the land* (Isaiah 1:19, NIV). God has so much good in store for us, in store for you; we just have to be willing to make the choice to do the work and be obedient to His Word.

If you are in a better position, if you have nothing stopping you from being all that you can be, and you are not putting your purpose to good use, it's an affront to God and the people who had to trudge their way to success. If you have a gift and decide not to use it for whatever reason, it's a tragedy. God will take away every obstacle, every trauma, every negative experience, every hindrance that's keeping a person from being where they need to be. But He will not move a person who insists on not being moved, who knows exactly what to do but chooses not to do it. That saying about not forcing a camel to drink water is true. God has taken you to the river; you need to bend down to drink.

Right now, you are probably thinking, *Okay, Shyra, we are not all cut out to be CEOs*. That's true.

God did not give everyone equal talents, but He gave every single one of us exactly what we need to excel, right where we are. Let me elaborate further with the story of the three servants with the talents.

The Parable of the Talents (Matthew 25:14-30, NRSVA)

A man was going on a journey. Before he left, he called his servants and entrusted his property to them. To one, he gave five talents, to another he gave two talents, and to the last, he gave one talent. He gave to each according to his ability. Then he went on his journey. Let's break this down.

It is strange, isn't it, that the man didn't give all the servants an equal share. There's nothing here that says one servant was greater or more senior than the other, but still, the man did not share his talents equally. It might seem strange, or even unfair, but it's not so strange when you understand that he gave them based on the servants' abilities. That's how we are with God.

There are some people who are just more talented than others. Some people appear to have more natural grace, charisma, luck, or whatever you want to call it than you. That thing they have more of is what God gave to them, and there's something you have more of that they don't. Have you ever met someone so kind, it stunned you? That's their talent. Not all talents come in the form of singing, dancing, or being math whizzes. God doesn't give us more than we can chew—far from it. He gives us our exact plate because He knows just how much impact we can make. Let's move on.

The servant who was given five talents went at once to trade with them, and he made five talents more. The servant who was given two talents went out and traded with them and made two more talents. But the servant with one talent went and dug a hole and hid his master's money.

What do you think was going through that servant's mind when he buried his talent? He was probably thinking, *Hey, all I've got is one talent; these people have way more than I do. Can you imagine? That other servant has a whole five talents. What am I supposed to do with one talent? I'm sure the master didn't want me to trade it anyway. Why? He has so much money. Not to mention all the interest he will get from the other talents. I am **comfortable**. I can live off what I already have.*

Okay, the servant didn't say that in the Bible, but you get where I'm going with this. I bet if that servant didn't have food, shelter, clothing, or anything to his name—if trading that talent was the only way he could survive—he would have made good on his talent. But even as a servant, he was comfortable.

Years passed, and the master came back to settle his accounts with his servants. The first servant came forward with his ten talents, and the master was pleased. He said, "Well done, good and faithful servant. You have been faithful over a little; I will set you over much." The second servant came with his four talents, and the master was also pleased. He said the same thing to him. But the third servant came with excuses. He said, "Master, I knew you to be a hard man, reaping where you did not sow, and gathering where you scattered no seed, so **I was afraid**, and I went and hid your talent in the ground. Here, you have what is yours."

Have you grown up with some form of entitlement? One where you think the gifts you have are too good to use? Do you think that by using your talents, you are depriving yourself of comfort, while the rest of the world enjoys it? Are you frustrated with your talent, thinking that God gave you something you don't want simply because He is trying to use you? Because that's what this servant thought. This servant who was given one talent, who was not given as many responsibilities and burdens as the others. He was given just one, and he still wouldn't use it. Perhaps the obstacles in front of you are not as big as you have made them seem, and perhaps like this servant, you are refusing to step out of your comfort zone. Well, here's what his master said to him:

"You wicked and slothful servant! You knew that I reap where I have not sown and gather where I scattered no seed? Then you ought to have invested my money with the bankers, and at my coming I should have received what was my own with interest." So the talent was taken from him and given to the one who had the ten talents.

I'll say it again. God has given each of us exactly what we need to excel right where we are. Stop burying your talent. STOP. BURYING. YOUR. TALENT. Stop burying it with excuses that we are not all going to be rich or famous or CEOs. Of course not! We all can't be. Excelling doesn't have to be about money or ambition; we've all been given gifts that can serve us and our immediate environment. It's like the Apostle Paul says:

In his grace, God has given us different gifts for doing certain things well. So if God has given you the ability to prophesy, speak out with as much faith as God has given you. If your gift is serving others, serve them well. If you are a teacher, teach well. If your gift is to encourage others, be encouraging. If it is giving, give generously. If God has given you leadership ability, take the responsibility seriously. And if you have a gift for showing kindness to others, do it gladly (Romans 12:6-8, NLT).

For instance, you could be great at teaching and imparting knowledge into young children, but you are forfeiting that to join the rat race in the corporate world.

You may be good at listening to people and helping them discern their feelings, but you won't give in to it because you are searching for someone else to be that for you.

You may be a naturally kind-hearted and warm person, but you have let the people of the world convince you that being kind means that others will walk all over you.

You may have the gift of service, the gift of helping others selflessly, but you have let society convince you never to give anything away for free.

You might be a beautiful singer. Perhaps your voice moves people, inspires them, or uplifts them. But you have convinced yourself that your church choir is beneath you, and if you don't perform on a worldwide scale, then you won't sing at all.

You might be a teacher that little boy needs, the one who is neglected, who comes to school hungry because his mother forgets to feed him. But even though you have the emotional and financial capability to give him what he needs, you don't because he's not your kid.

We all have that one thing the world around us needs. Some people have it more, some people have it less, but we all have just enough to create, to touch, to inspire.

Don't be like the third servant. Don't stay so comfortable, so entitled, so afraid that you bury your talent and let it go to waste.

Every single one of us will give an account of what we have been given. Don't be the one who disappoints God and yourself.

In our next section, we are going to look at practical steps to healing and becoming the you God wants you to be. Buckle up!

PART 2

CHAPTER 7

IT'S NOT YOUR FAULT, BUT IT IS YOUR RESPONSIBILITY

Here's the thing about fault and responsibility: people want to draw a straight line from one to the other. People want to believe that the only reason you should fix something is if it was your fault. No one wants to be burdened with the responsibility of fixing something they didn't break, especially if the blame rests squarely on someone else. Good thing Jesus wasn't thinking like this; if He was, we would still be covered in sins caused by our faults, and there would be no uniting us with The Father.

I know you want to stay mad at your parents, at your spouse, at your abuser, or at society forever. Because holding on to that anger or grudge is a burden, and it's one you are okay with bearing. It's a comfortable, familiar burden fueled by fervent, righteous anger. You want your abuser to own up to their actions. You want them to say, "Look, it's my fault. I'm sorry and I'm going to fix it." But here's the reality of the situation. They may never take the blame or admit to the wrongs, and it's almost always impossible for them to "fix it."

Consider an eighteen-year-old foster child who has aged out of the system doesn't wait for their parents to come get them, no matter how much they wish that would happen. Once they come of age, they grab their backpack and go face the big world for themselves. It was not their fault they were placed in the system, and they certainly didn't ask to be born. But at that moment, at that age, it becomes their responsibility to make something of themselves. And they certainly aren't walking into a society ready to love and accept them with open arms.

So, if that scared eighteen-year-old can face the world with just a backpack, then why can't you face the wreck in your life that your parents made?

If someone sets your house on fire and walks away, would you wait for them to come back and put it out, or would you grab an extinguisher and get to work? But it's the arsonist's fault, isn't it? So why not let your house burn to the ground? Because it's your house, not theirs. It's your life, not your parents'. So no matter how you twist it, no matter how badly you want to blame someone else for the experiences that shaped your life, that hurt or broke you, and no matter how much they deserve that blame, the core truth remains: you are in charge of your destiny, and that makes you responsible for fixing your life. No matter what your parents have done to you, no matter the upbringing you have had, it is your responsibility to activate the blessing of choice to do and be better.

Most people frown at the responsibility of fixing their life because they think taking it on immediately makes the problem their fault. But that is shortsighted. If, in some twisted way, you think taking responsibility for your life is going to make anyone see your circumstances as your fault, then you are living in a very toxic bubble, and you need to get out of it before it chokes you. Do you honestly believe anyone is going to blame you for having a toxic mother? Of course not! And even if they did, the problem is with them, not you. But do you think anyone is going to congratulate you for spending the rest of your life faulting your mother? No. If they do, they're wrong. As a child, you had no choice, but as an adult, you own your choices and mistakes.

Yes, you had a traumatic childhood, and yes, absolutely, your trauma is validated. But you can no longer lay the blame at the feet of your parents with cries of "It's your fault! Fix me!" Many abusive parents are not even aware they were ever abusive, and the more you blame them as an adult, the more they are going to look at you as a spoiled, petulant, ungrateful child.

Assigning fault keeps you stuck in the past, doing the blame dance and being a victim. Taking responsibility catapults you to the present. It keeps you alert and aware, and it will have you actively seeking opportunities that will make your life better. So, would you rather blame or be responsible? Do you want to be that hurt little child forever, or do you want to be a healed and thriving adult?

Recovering from Childhood Trauma: Let the Healing Begin

Will I ever recover from my childhood? That's the question people with the most devastating childhoods ask. They fear they are too far gone. But I'll say it again: there's nothing so broken that God can't fix it, nothing so tangled that He cannot untangle. God is a miracle worker, THE MIRACLE WORKER, and all He's ever asked of us is to trust and obey. To trust that He can turn your childhood around, and then obey His direction for your life.

I know you are afraid to take that next step. You are afraid to trust, afraid of failing, afraid of being mocked for daring to do things differently and better. But "Cast all your anxiety on Him, because He cares for you" (1 Peter 5:7, NIV).

Steps to Recovering from Childhood Trauma

Acknowledge and Accept the Truth

This is where it began for me. The hardest part of recovering from childhood trauma was to recognize and accept the truth for what it was and what it still is.

I knew something was wrong, something all the way down to my childhood. I knew I was unhappy, unfulfilled, directionless, and afraid, but I did not want to claim the tag "traumatized" for many reasons. I thought, *Suck it up! Many people have terrible childhoods. Yours wasn't even that bad.* But here's the thing: Many situations and experiences we and our ancestors had to deal with were so normalized, we didn't even realize how damaging they were. It wasn't until I began my walk with God that I began to see patterns and toxic beliefs that were limiting me. God opened my eyes, and then it became impossible for me not to acknowledge my situation. It's one thing for God to open your eyes, and it's another thing for you to accept what He's shown you.

Acknowledging the truth about your trauma can be hard. But, as you already know, the past doesn't always stay in the past. Whether or not you acknowledge it, the symptoms of your trauma will shadow you wherever you go. It's imperative that you acknowledge it. But first, you need to recognize the trauma.

Not all trauma symptoms are glaring, but these questions should help root them out:

- Are you detached and apathetic from situations that should elicit sympathy and empathy?
- Are you nonchalant over things you should be concerned about?
- Are you intensely pessimistic?

- Do you get angry and explosive over issues that don't require that kind of reaction?
- Have you lost your faith in God?
- Do you get anxious or stressed over big or small situations?
- Do you find it hard to connect to or trust people?

Once you recognize these symptoms in yourself, then you need to accept that you need help and healing. Your parents' unresolved issues from their childhood were theirs to acknowledge and heal, just like yours are. When a parent doesn't recognize, acknowledge, and accept the truth of their unresolved issues, they'll only do the best they can with what they know.

Mourn

You will be surprised at how intense the feeling of sadness will be. For me, it was like nothing I had ever experienced before. All my life, I had somehow assumed that my mother's actions toward me were my fault, that I had done something to deserve them. I had taken the brunt of my mother's actions on myself, sometimes excusing her behavior, other times blaming myself for not doing or being what she wanted me to be. But the moment I acknowledged my symptoms, I saw the abusive relationship had been going on for years. All these years, she had been hurting me without her or me fully knowing or understanding it. So I mourned, for the mother I wished she had been and for the years of ignorance I had lived in. I started to forgive myself, and very importantly, I started to forgive her.

But in mourning, I not only realized what I had lost, but also what I stood to gain if I followed the right direction. You will be tempted to stay in your mourning period for longer than you should, but don't. It's okay to allow these emotions to wash through you, but don't let them sink you.

Remember that joy does come in the morning, but it won't if you won't even try to go to sleep.

Reclaim Your Life

The more I acknowledged my trauma and learned about it, the more I realized how easy it was to get stuck in the victim mentality. Sure, being a victim will garner you sympathy, but for how long? It's only a matter of time before people start to expect you to get on with your life, to make a change and heal. You can allow that victim status to hold you down and prevent you from living your life, or you can take the necessary steps to reclaim and live the life you want to live. The devil loves a victim. He hides their relief in self-pity and stops them from seeing or utilizing their power. But you can't allow the devil to keep you fetching and bathing from a well of self-pity, not when God has fresh, clean water waiting for you. You can't allow the past to hold you prisoner; that's a sentence you should not be serving. You and only you have to break the chain of what's holding you down. Once you do the work to heal the pain in your life, you begin to develop the courage and strength of stepping into control and obtaining the blessings in life that belong to you. And how can you reclaim your life?

Renew Your Mind

You HAVE to stop thinking and processing actions like a victim. You were a victim then, but no more. You need to accept the truth of what God has spoken over you, and the first place to start is immersing yourself in His word. Don't let anyone tell you who you are, not when God has perfectly defined you. Say it to yourself, as loud as you should, as much as you need to: I AM NOT A VICTIM. The devil cannot claim what you don't give him. Sure, he can traumatize you, but he can't take your self-worth, and he certainly can't stop you from healing unless you offer your healing to him on a platter of self-pity.

Find the Right Resource

Reclaiming your life will not happen in a vacuum. Also, if you have been far from God and His word for a long time, you are going to need help getting back. So, pray and ask God to lead you to the right person to help you with this. There will be many people claiming they can help, but only the God-directed can help you. Don't just tell your story to anyone; ask God to lead you to the right people who will not only validate your pain but offer you the right resources to heal.

Seek Professional Help

Don't listen to the lies you've been told; therapy is not for the weak. It is for people who are strong enough to take charge of their life. God has provided us with many resources on this earth to help us heal from our trauma. And what's more, He's right there with us as we go on our journey. Find a mental health expert who is rooted in the Word so they can begin guiding you to reclaim your life.

Secure Your Support System

When I took steps to recover from my trauma, my mother hurt me, a lot. My distance and healing were an affront to her. There's one thing you must understand: often, the people who caused your trauma will be the ones most against your recovery from it. The best thing you can do is steer clear of them and find yourself a group that supports you. There's comfort in knowing that you did not suffer this alone, that there are others like you who get it. A significant part of my healing was connecting with others who had similar experiences. The strange thing was, I actually never went to find these people. God has an amazing way of bringing the right people to you at the right time.

The best thing about finding a support system is that they will provide you with tips on how to get through it. They will tell you what worked for them, what didn't, and why. I know there's this urge to keep your business private, to not let people know what's going on in your life so they don't judge you for it. But strength can be found in community. The more you talk about your experiences and listen to those of others, the more hope you will have. You will even begin to see that your situation is not so terrible. Once I was able to get through talking about it without crying, I knew things were looking up for me.

Unlearn and Relearn

Be prepared to learn that much of what you've considered truth throughout your life is likely a lie. Many of us grew up with thoughts and beliefs that were not truly our own, but rather beliefs and thoughts that were imposed upon us through teachings or negative experiences. The first thing to recognize is that you are responsible for your own happiness. You cannot rely on another person or external things to make you happy; true happiness is found within yourself and in your relationship with God.

Taking the time to learn and explore things for yourself is crucial to breaking free from the bonds of false beliefs. Learning is an ongoing process that requires regular updates, much like a computer needing software updates to function efficiently. If you choose to remain stagnant throughout your life without embracing change, growth, and self-improvement, it will be challenging to attain a fulfilling life. I had to unlearn old limiting beliefs and replace them with new, empowering ones. I discovered that the renewal of the mind is a powerful tool that can lead you to the life you truly deserve to live.

Here's something new you should learn: If you've ever thought you were worthless, let the words of Ephesians 2:10 dispel that lie. If you believed your worth was determined by your actions and contributions, remember that Jesus's selfless sacrifice on the cross means you can come as you are. If you thought change was impossible, let my transformation serve as a testimony that change is indeed possible. To embrace this transformation, you must be open to unlearning old beliefs and relearning new ones.

How can you do this?

Be Open-Minded

Accept the fact that there's much you don't know and that there are better possibilities for you. Acknowledge that what you've been doing hasn't yielded the desired results, and it's time to try something different. An open heart and mind are essential for learning and growth.

Learn from Others

Understand that there are millions of people who have experienced situations similar to yours, survived, and emerged stronger. I am a prime example of this. If you ever doubt that things can change or believe you can't improve your life, look to those who have walked the path before you. Sometimes God allows us and others to go through challenges so we can learn and grow from them. Rather than doubting ourselves or judging others, we should seek lessons in these experiences.

Be Intentional

The past will always cast a shadow, tempting you to revert to old habits. Counter this by being intentional. Be mindful of the words you speak and the company you keep. Use positive affirmations and declare God's promises over your life. Words hold power, and the influence of your social circle is significant. Surround yourself with people who support your journey, and speak positivity into your life. The more you immerse yourself in a positive environment, the more likely you are to reach your goals.

Take Care of You

On your journey to healing, you will experience months of doubt, anxiety, depression, and perhaps even moments of self-hate. You will question whether you are making the right choices; recovering from childhood trauma can feel like you're exposing your family's issues. It might seem as though you are passing judgment or suddenly considering yourself superior to them. You might even struggle with insomnia as you spend nights immersed in thoughts.

During these challenging moments, it's crucial to prioritize self-care and learn to take care of yourself. It may feel selfish, but it's essential to put yourself first.

You must invest in your well-being before you can effectively support others.

While you may be tempted to stay busy as a coping mechanism, it's important not to overdo it. Instead, give yourself permission to pause and breathe. I, too, attempted to stay busy as a coping strategy, but it ultimately had negative effects.

Over time, I discovered the importance of slowing down and finding joy in life's small moments. I realized that if I continued to run myself down, I wouldn't be able to offer my best self to my husband and children. I learned the value of taking naps and establishing calming morning routines instead of rushing into the day.

Be Patient with Yourself

Healing won't happen in the first month, the second month, or even the first year. Reclaiming and renewing your mind is a lifelong process that requires daily commitment. So, if you don't experience immediate changes or feel instantly liberated, understand that you are on the right path, and it takes time. When it gets too overwhelming, when you start to fear that you can't do it, let the words of Isaiah 41:10, NIV calm you: *So do not fear, for I am with you; do not be dismayed, for I am your God. I will strengthen you and help you; I will uphold you with my righteous right hand.*

God wants us to do the necessary work to truly get to know Him, live well, and bring Him glory. The Bible tells us to come to Him, cast our burdens on

Him, and He will sustain us. The Bible also tells us that we will face troubles and challenges, and life can be difficult, but in Him, we can find peace. This is exactly what happened during my healing process. He was there and continues to be there, protecting me and granting me a peace that can only come from Him. I have no doubt that He will do the same for you.

CHAPTER 8

BREAKING GENERATIONAL PATTERNS AND BEHAVIORS: YOU ARE NOT YOUR PARENTS

"The apple doesn't fall far from the tree" is a popular saying often repeated by two types of people: those who lack reasons or examples to believe otherwise and those who find comfort in blaming their life choices on their parents or genetics. However, if there's one thing this book has emphasized, it's that we are children of God. While humans may speak words over you based on past experiences, God speaks words over you based on your future. He exists outside of time, having seen different versions of you, and He knows that you only become like your parents if you follow in their footsteps, rather than the path He has set for you.

I understand that there have been generations who endured similar experiences and now lead challenging lives, making it seem like a curse to you. However, you are not them; you are unique. They are the way they are because they didn't put in the work, didn't know how to, or perhaps didn't have the opportunity to change their circumstances. But it can all change with you, and it begins with one crucial step:

Become the Cycle Breaker

A cycle breaker stands out as the exception. They are the person within the family who boldly declares, "Enough! It stops with me!" A cycle breaker is someone who recognizes the dysfunction within the family, the repetition of destructive patterns, and makes a conscious effort to change them. They are the individuals who tap into their personal power, their unique identity, distancing themselves from the family's established image. They commit to self-improvement and meaningful change.

Many people mistakenly believe that familial traits and habits are purely genetic, comparing them to inheriting physical characteristics like bad eyesight from one's mother or height from one's father. This misconception leads them to think that toxic familial cycles are hereditary, making it seem impossible to break free because it's "in the blood" or because "the apple doesn't fall far from the tree," or even because of the "nature over nurture" argument. However, familial cycles are more a result of learned behavior than genetics. While there are genetic traits passed down from parents, such as physical characteristics, the truly toxic traits are often those we have observed, mimicked, and internalized. The good news is that learned behavior can be unlearned with practice and time.

Being a cycle breaker is an arduous journey. It is far from a quick fix. It begins with a deep understanding of why your family behaves the way it does. In some cases, these patterns may be so deeply ingrained in traits and behaviors that uncovering them requires significant effort. It may involve dismantling the facade of a seemingly perfect family to expose the destructive patterns that have taken hold. It might require distancing yourself from the family temporarily to focus on your own personal growth and development.

Many families remain unaware that they are trapped in a toxic cycle. Consider, for instance, a family of overachievers. To the outside world, they appear to be successful individuals, conquering their respective worlds. But a closer look might reveal burnt-out adults trapped in jobs they despise, driven by the need for validation from their parents or others in their circle. Even the most seemingly perfect exterior can hide an underlying sense of emptiness. You can't solely rely on appearances or emotions; you must pray to God for discernment.

If you choose to believe that you were born with these tendencies and can't overcome the anchor weighing you down, you are denying yourself the power to change. Do not evade the toxicity that is holding you back. Do not attribute it to genetics or biology. While certain traits may be genetic, traumas and generational patterns are learned behaviors. They are called "patterns" because they can be unlearned. Ignoring these issues will only lead to stumbling over them repeatedly. You must make a courageous decision to become the cycle breaker.

Initially, it may feel shameful to even entertain the thought that your family is toxic and that action is needed. This realization can challenge your sense of loyalty and self-identity. You may believe you are betraying your family just by considering taking action. Furthermore, your family might perceive you as an enemy and react with attacks, ridicule, or isolation. They may attempt to pull you back into the fold by undermining your progress. Do not allow this to deter you. Many positive transformations begin in challenging circumstances.

As you embark on this journey of change and enlightenment, you might grapple with the idea of changing your parents, grandparents, or whoever you believe initiated the cycle. It may take some time to realize that you are only responsible for your own actions and decisions. You can't change anyone who is unwilling to change, nor can you fix someone determined to break. Instead, focus on yourself and ask these crucial questions: Can I be better? Can I do better? Do I want my children to experience the same childhood and adulthood I've had?

Most families go through generations and generations before finding that cycle breaker, that person who's had enough. Let yours be you.

How to Become the Cycle Breaker
Identify the Problem

The first step in solving any problem is identifying it. As I highlighted in Chapter Five, generational patterns are not always obvious. Sometimes, even when they are apparent, we are the last ones to recognize them. To become the cycle breaker, start by carefully observing what needs to change. If necessary, write it down. Examine the recurring patterns within your family and trace their origins. Analyze how frequently they occur, who is affected, and the underlying reasons.

For instance, you might have observed that your uncle, his father, and his grandfather were all alcoholics. Instead of accepting this as a given, take the time to sit down with your uncle and ask him why he drinks excessively. Perhaps you are on the verge of a divorce, just like your mother and her mother before her. Before finalizing any decisions, approach your mother and inquire, "Why is it that the women in our family rarely stay in marriages?"

Do not ignore the issues by dismissing them as if they are insignificant. Doing so is akin to standing on train tracks, waiting for an impending collision. Do not say, "So what? Every family has its quirks." While that may be true, your family's patterns are the anchor that is holding you down. If you refuse to acknowledge the existence of a problem, you will remain trapped within it, and it will become your children's problem as well. You must loathe the toxic cycle within your family so intensely that you don't merely want to break it—you want to obliterate it.

Listen and Understand

After identifying these patterns, you should make an effort to understand them. It's crucial to clarify that understanding does not equate to excusing bad behavior. Rather, you seek to understand it so that you can prevent it from recurring. When you delve deeply into the root causes of these issues, you gain valuable insights and a sense of direction, enabling you to formulate a plan.

Consider your parents and, if possible, their parents in an attempt to comprehend their traumas. Ask them what shaped them into the individuals they are today. Did they raise you as they did because it mirrored their own upbringing? Did they inflict pain on you because they were themselves hurting? It's important to bear in mind that your parents or grandparents may not be as receptive as you hope. No one willingly submits themselves to examination, and no one wishes to feel as though something is inherently wrong with them. Therefore, when you approach your parents or your abuser, whoever it may be, try to avoid coming across as confrontational. Instead, approach the situation with humility and compassion. Remember that, regardless of the circumstances, you are in a privileged position—a chance to address and rectify your issues—a position they, for some reason, may have never had.

Avoid entering the discussion with anger. I initially wanted to remain furious at my mother, wondering how someone in a role with such a significant impact on a person's life could become the source of so much pain. Eventually, by God's grace, I realized I could choose to remain angry or take the time to understand and heal.

As you make the effort to understand, remember that you don't have to allow someone to continue hurting you. If they persist in causing you harm, consider distancing yourself from them. In one way or another, God will provide you with the answers you need.

Accept What You Know and What You Cannot Change

Some truths are very hard to accept, and some people are very hard to change. The more you learn about your family, the more challenging it may be to accept certain truths. For example, you might discover that your mother was mean to you not because her mother was mean to her, but because that's just her personality. Or, you might find out that your father abused you because he experienced similar abuse from his own father. Learning these truths about your parents can elicit feelings of hatred or empathy from you.

If a parent opens up to you in this way, it's essential not to judge them or attempt to change them, as you cannot do so. The best course of action is to accept and empathize with their experiences. This process may be difficult, and it won't happen overnight, but it's necessary for your own personal growth and healing.

When I learned about the unfortunate experiences my mother had endured during her early years in life, I realized how blessed and favored I was. I could never imagine myself having to go through some of the experiences she endured. As a result, I've accepted the truth of what has happened and can now choose to approach it from a place of understanding.

Forgive

The words of Luke 6: 37, NIV fit so perfectly here. *Do not judge, and you will not be judged. Do not condemn, and you will not be condemned. Forgive, and you will be forgiven.*

We all fall into the trap of thinking that, given the opportunity, we would do things differently. However, there's a reason why God allowed me to go through the trauma I experienced and not the kind my mother did. Perhaps it was because He knew my mother could survive it, but I wouldn't have been able to. God doesn't give us more than we can handle; He appoints us to use our experiences and stories of triumph to help others.

Forgiveness may seem easy in theory, but putting it into practice can be challenging. How can you forgive someone who has spent their whole life hurting you? Doesn't forgiving them make you weak? No, it doesn't. In fact, being able to forgive is one of the most powerful acts in the world, and only a person who has been empowered by God can truly achieve it.

Holding onto a grudge is like being stranded at sea or walking around with a dark cloud over your head. When you don't forgive, you bear the burden of what has been done to you, in addition to the pain it caused. Some people fear that forgiving their wrongdoer would absolve them of their sins, but your forgiveness doesn't have the power to do that. It only frees you from carrying that heavy burden. The person who has wronged you still carries the weight of their actions, whether they acknowledge it or not. Until they seek forgiveness from you and from God, they will continue to carry that weight.

For me, reaching the point of forgiveness was not easy, but I knew it was necessary to release myself from carrying the burden. The toxic behavior I endured from my mother left me with deep emotional wounds, but I couldn't allow it to define me. The forgiveness I chose to give was not for her; it was something I had to do for myself. Forgiving her actions didn't mean I blindly trusted her again; trust had to be earned. It simply meant that I had to set myself free from the pain and move forward into the future, embracing the life God had in store for me.

Set Boundaries

To embark on your journey toward healing and breaking those toxic cycles, you must establish boundaries. You must sever the relationship that has you and your family trapped in that cycle. Setting boundaries is incredibly crucial, especially because your family may not understand or support your decision. They might antagonize and attack you. It may be a challenging period for you, but you need to remain steadfast. Setting those boundaries doesn't mean you don't forgive them, and it certainly doesn't mean you don't love and support them; quite the opposite. You can love and support them from a distance.

Another reason why you need to establish boundaries is if the abuse is still ongoing. A wound that is constantly poked does not heal. Although I forgave my mother, I realized I had to immediately establish boundaries with her. She was still toxic and abusive, and I knew that if I were to heal, I could not be around her. You know what I've learned? When it's a parent who has been abusing you, and you are trying to set boundaries with them, people may say, "Oh, but he's your father" or "But she's your mother. You can't do that to them." But consider this: if your husband or wife were physically abusing you, and you made the decision to leave or set boundaries with them, would people tell you to stay with them and keep allowing them to harm you physically? Of course not! They would encourage you to distance yourself from the abuse and support your decision, even if it led to a divorce.

Before you get worried, setting boundaries is not unchristian. The words of Hebrews 12:1, NIV reinforces the need to set boundaries so that we don't get entangled in the sin that hinders us. It says, *Therefore, since we are surrounded by such a great cloud of witnesses, let us throw off everything that hinders and the sin that so easily entangles. And let us run with perseverance the race marked out for us.* This sin doesn't have to be yours. As long as it hinders God's calling for your life, as long as it impedes your recovery, construct the strongest boundary possible and stand resolutely behind it. Here are a few methods to establish boundaries:

Take Time Away From Those Who Cause You Pain

Do it like your life depends on it, because it does. If you have to cut off communication for a while, do it. Then come back when you know their words and actions won't have as much effect on you. Another reason you should take time away from those who hurt you is that you need to discover who you are, apart from or without them. This will be uncomfortable at first, and it may even feel like you are going to extremes. But whenever that thought crosses your mind, let the words of Hebrews 12:1 reassure you.

Learn to Say NO

After you step away, naturally, toxic family members will try to reel you back in. They will whine, guilt, cajole, and even threaten you. But no matter how they do it, no matter what they say, as long as it goes contrary to your healing, your answer should be a firm "No."

Find Support

When you step away, you might feel lonely and maybe a little isolated. That's why you need a strong community to assure you that you are doing the right thing. The more you are around them, the less lonely you will feel in your journey.

Renew Your Mind

This is the moment where you begin to fill your mind with all the right things. Empty it of the lies, and fill it with God's truth. Empty it of your doubts, and fill it with God's certainties. Empty it of your weaknesses, and fill it with God's strength. Day by day, be intentional about the words you speak over yourself, about the content you let into your heart, and about the people you keep around you.

It is very easy to backslide, to fall back into the old ways and go back to being part of the cycle. That's why you have to take God's hand on your journey. The truth is, you can't renew your mind on your own;

only God can do it for you, and all He wants is your permission.

Every step listed here is giving God permission to renew your mind, to turn your grave of hurt and shame into a garden of blessings and healing. And in giving that permission, you know what I've realized? We don't have to stay stuck in the patterns we were brought up in. Those patterns don't define who we are. We can become the model of the new desired pattern, a reflection of the legacy we wish to leave behind for ourselves and our children. I wish for my legacy to display love and kindness.

Right here, in this moment, you can think of yourself as one of two things: an individual with the power to make choices and decisions that shape their life, or an individual who believes their actions and choices are shaped by the actions and inactions of their parents. Which is it going to be?

CHAPTER 9

RIDDING YOURSELF OF LIMITING CHILDHOOD BELIEFS

When you're a small child, your parents are almost like gods to you. They tell you what to eat and where to go. They lay down laws and rules that guide your interaction with them and others. It's their belief in you and of you that leads you to form yours about yourself. So, when your mom says you are stupid or not deserving of good things, even if it feels wrong to you, it will also feel right. It doesn't immediately occur to you to seek a different belief. If your parents, the people who birthed you, think this low of you, why should anyone else think differently? Much less a God you don't even see. But, that's what I need you to consider right now, that God you don't see, the one who's felt far from you for the longest time. I want you to take a deep breath, close your eyes, and ask yourself, what does God believe about me?

Cognitive dissonance is a theory developed by Leon Festinger in the 1950s that suggests inconsistencies about what we believe about ourselves, our environment, or the world lead to discomfort. Essentially, having conflicting beliefs about something important to us makes us very uncomfortable. We like it when our beliefs and resulting actions and consequences align.

For instance, if you believe you are good at math but keep failing at it, this will unnerve you—your mind is saying one thing, but your results are thwarting that belief, so your mind will do something to align this inconsistency. Either you will decide that you are good at math and work hard at it, or you will conclude that you aren't and keep failing at it. One way or another, your mind will align your belief to give you some measure of peace. It will also help you explain away things that thwart this peace of mind. If you believe you are bad at relationships, every time you go into one, you will expect it to end badly. To explain your trail of bad relationships, you will simply point to what you believe: *My relationships fail because I'm bad at them.*

If you grew up believing you were undeserving of love, then every time someone treats you in an unloving way, it aligns with what you already believe. And if you find someone who treats you with love, it will shock you and unearth the balance of belief you've come to know and accept. So you reject them or subconsciously try to sabotage the relationship because the result is inconsistent with your belief.

The point is when our belief and behavior, or other people's behavior, toward us don't align, we have to change one of them in order to have peace. It's who we are, how we are wired. Your belief influences your actions. If you believe you are a good person, you will do things that a good person would do. If you believe you are a bad person, you will align your actions with that.

All your life, your decisions and actions have aligned with your belief, a belief you internalized as a child. One that was fueled by the actions and inactions of your parents and the environment around you.

So you came to believe that you are worthless, undeserving of love or good things. You came to believe you don't need redemption, so when something wrong or awful happens to you, you agree with it. In fact, you've come to expect it.

You came to believe there's no escaping the cycle your family is so caught up in; that there is no healing from your trauma. You've walked, you've breathed, you've lived in these beliefs. They've become your truth, your reality.

Forget what you believe about yourself, and ask yourself this question:

What does God believe about me?

That's the only question that matters; it's the only one that ever has.

With cognitive dissonance, we seek to align our beliefs with our actions. But what if we didn't do that? What if, instead, we aligned our actions with God's beliefs about us?

I had many limiting beliefs as an adult, beliefs that stemmed from my relationship with my mother when I was a child. Growing up, I was not a frivolous or demanding child; there was no room for that. But even with the few and basic things I got, I always felt like I wasn't deserving of them or I was a burden because of the way my mother reacted every time I asked for things I needed. At fifteen I got myself a job and felt a deep sense of relief. Also by this time, I had already internalized this belief that I didn't deserve things and that the only things I deserved were things I worked myself to the bone for. So, when blessings came to me—blessings I didn't necessarily work for—it was hard for me to accept them. A part of me was certain I didn't deserve them, and the other part was afraid these blessings wouldn't last.

It was hard to believe that God is a good Father, a good and perfect Father who blesses us not because we deserve it, but because He loves us. The book of John 11:41 tells us that God blesses us despite our flaws—flaws that even our earthly parents could not possibly get over. God never guilted me for what He gave me. He never made me feel like I did not deserve them. He gives because He loves to give. God gives even to the people who don't believe in Him. And what's more,

He doesn't give us what we want; He gives us what's perfect for us.

I had several other limiting beliefs that resulted from childhood experiences. For instance, I experienced trust issues and difficulty asking for things I needed, and there was also the feeling of not being good enough. I had faced intense criticism, judgment, and shaming. These beliefs restricted me and made it hard for me to fully try or go after what I wanted. To overcome these beliefs, I had to shift my way of thinking to a more empowering and truthful one, God's. The moment I did, the things I believed about myself began to expose themselves for the lies they were.

One thing I've learned is that if we rely on our own directions, if we rely on our worth or beliefs about ourselves, we will continue to stumble. That is why we have to shift our way of thinking from *This is what I believe about myself* to *This is what God believes about me*. The moment you align your behaviors with God's beliefs about you, your life will change in amazing ways.

I should know. Mine has!

This brings us to an obvious question: how? How do I shift my focus from what I believe about myself to what God believes about me?

Write Down Your Beliefs

What do you believe about yourself? Take a moment, sit down, grab a piece of paper and a pen, and write it down. Some limiting beliefs can be so deeply internalized that we may not even be aware of them until we engage in some deep soul-searching.

However, if delving too deeply into this feels overwhelming right now, start on the surface. Identify some surface-level beliefs about what you think you can't do or don't deserve. These might be things that appear normal to you and everyone around you, negative traits that everyone has come to accept about you. For instance, when you leave a relationship after a few weeks, do your friends say, "You're just not very good at relationships"? Have you ever attempted something positive only to have a close friend comment, "What, you? You're usually terrible at that!" Sometimes it's these seemingly harmless beliefs that limit us. It's the things your friends may attribute to your personality, normality, or even your zodiac sign, like saying, "I'm a Capricorn, so I can't stick to a job," or "I'm a Leo, so I don't forgive easily."

Writing out your limiting beliefs will bring clarity. You might not fully grasp the extent of what you believe about yourself until you see it on paper. Moreover, simply writing them down can be the first step toward changing those beliefs. Imagine this: you've just put in writing that you don't believe you deserve love. Doesn't that alarm you?

Explore Their Root

Now, play detective. Ask yourself (and anyone else you need to) how you came to believe these negative things about yourself. In my case, I could draw a straight line from my beliefs back to my childhood and the influence my parents had on me. Some of us have formed limiting beliefs based on isolated incidents. One negative event occurred, one person hurt you, and you generalized it. Essentially, you turned minor issues into major obstacles. What you did, in effect, was deny your ability to give and receive second chances.

Some of us have shaped our beliefs based on the opinions of others, simply because they hold a certain authority or influence over us. However, the only influence and authority we should be subject to are God's. It's like believing that love doesn't exist, not because you've experienced heartbreak, but because you've seen someone else go through it. It's like pouring your entire pot of soup down the drain because your neighbor five blocks away found a roach in theirs.

Once you explore and identify the root of your limiting beliefs, it becomes easier to uproot and replace them.

Recognize Their Effect

Now, draw a straight line from that belief to everything you've lost.

Because you believe you aren't deserving of love, you've spent your life chasing after partners who gave you only the bare minimum. Because you believe you don't deserve success, you settled for jobs that made you miserable. Because you feared rejection, you let countless opportunities slip through your fingers. Because you believe you have no control over your life or circumstances, you've simply let life happen to you. Because you believe you deserve to be alone, you didn't fight to save your marriage. Because you believe you don't deserve forgiveness, you've carried around a heavy burden of guilt. Because you don't believe you are valuable, you've allowed people to treat you like trash. The list goes on and on.

Your limiting beliefs keep you from changing your world and the worlds of the people around you. For every negative thing you believe about yourself, there's a resulting effect, and you are not the only one who suffers the consequences.

Uproot and Replant

Your beliefs were planted in toxic soil, and as a result, everything that grew out of it was bad. But no more of that. This question is about how you uproot and replant. So, ask yourself again: What does God believe about me?

Here, let me help:

- God believes that you are valuable. He said, *The very hairs on your head are all numbered* (Matthew 10:30, NIV).
- God believes you are worthy of love. He affirms this by saying, *For I know the plans I have for you…They are plans for good and not for disaster, to give you a future and a hope* (Jeremiah

29:11, NLT). He loves you so much, He has a whole future planned for you.
- God believes in your power because He gave it to you. Paul attested to this when he said, *For I can do everything through Christ, who gives me strength* (Philippians 4:13, NLT).
- God believes you are unique and perfect the way you are. David was so moved when he realized this that he said, *Thank you for making me so wonderfully complex! Your workmanship is marvelous—how well I know it* (Psalm 139:14, NLT).

God believes all of this about you and more. The entire Bible is a testament to how much God values you because its entire story leads up to one moment: the one where Jesus died for you.

Write Down New Beliefs

Our cognitive dissonance seeks to align our beliefs with our actions, but forget that. Write down what God believes about you and align your actions with that. God thinks you are fearfully and wonderfully made; act accordingly. God thinks you are forgiven, so drop the guilt. Why carry a burden that Jesus has already taken for you? God thinks you are valuable and worth all the love there is to give, so don't put yourself in situations with people who don't see you the way God does. You need to see who God sees every time you look in the mirror. You need to see the wonder He sees.

So, take a pen and paper and write it down. Every word, every promise God has spoken about your life. God is not a God of limitations, not where His love is concerned. He will break down walls and mountains to find you. He will leave the ninety-nine to come get you (Matthew 18:10-14).

Write it down. Write down how much you are loved, because you are. Write down how beautifully imperfect you are, because in God's eyes, you are. Write down how, despite your flaws, God still loves and wants you, because He does. Write down how brave and courageous you are because God has not given you a spirit of fear. Write down how you are not alone because God walks with you and comforts you. Write down your plans, no matter how big and impossible, because your God is a God of impossibilities. Write down how you don't have to fear the future because God's plans for you are good and never evil. They are plans to give you hope and a beautiful future. Write down how you are not forsaken or abandoned because God is always with you.

What your earthly parents say doesn't matter, especially when their words are filled with hate and negativity. No, because before they were your parents, you were a child of God. Where they can't love you, where they don't see the wonder that you are, God saw it even before He created and formed you. He has known you even before they did.

Shyra Smith

So, what do their beliefs matter? What power does your limiting belief have over you when God, the sovereign creator, knows you, loves you, and calls you by name? When His beliefs about you are full of limitless, boundless, and beautiful possibilities?

CHAPTER 10

WORK, TRUST, AND OBEY

You have all that you need to transition from the pain of your trauma to the fruits of your healing. This book has pointed you in the right direction, and the Bible contains everything you will ever need to know to grow and thrive.

Now all you have to do is work, trust, and obey.

Work

Ah, "work," such a tiring and, to some, degrading word. I know what you're thinking: God is a God of miracles, isn't He? He parted the sea, He raised the dead back to life, He multiplied fish and bread, and there was that time when He turned water into wine. So, couldn't He just touch you and move you from point A to B? Couldn't He just heal you from your trauma so you can move on with your life? Well, He can. Absolutely,

He can. But there are situations where God needs you to show up, and this journey is one of them.

You see, God wants you to put in the work, not grudgingly but intentionally. You have to do it because you want to, because you are willing, not because someone is making you do it. You have to do it because you hate where you are right now and want it to change. You have to do it for yourself. God is ready to help; He always is. You just have to show Him that you're ready and you want to be helped.

I'm not going to sugarcoat it for you; the work is hard, very hard, especially in the beginning. I know because I struggled with putting in the work and following through. Staying on the healing wagon seemed like enormous work. I didn't believe that I could simply create boundaries. In fact, it's safe to say I didn't have much confidence in the beginning. I had this Bible verse, though: *For I can do everything through Christ, who gives me strength* (Philippians 4:13, NLT). If you are going to succeed at this work, you just might need that verse on repeat. If you are going to stay disciplined and put in the work the right way, you'll need to pray and ask God to guide you, to give you the strength and confidence to move forward with this journey.

In the beginning, it will be easy to convince yourself that the work doesn't matter. You will move from excitement at the prospect of your new, enriching life to depressing nonchalance—because what's the point anyway, especially when you realize just how much work you'll need to put in. That's exactly how it was for me. The work terrified me so much that I almost gave up. One thing I've learned is that God will meet you where you are, but He will not drag you, not when He knows you can get up and walk with Him. God wants you to put in the work, not because He can't do it for you but because He knows doing it yourself will improve your character. It's just like with your child. You know you can do that science project for them in thirty minutes. But you let them spend all weekend working on it because in doing it themselves, they gain experience. They learn how to do it and are able to take pride in what they have accomplished.

Another thing you are going to need to accomplish this work is discipline. I have met people who claim to want to do the work, who know exactly what to do to get better, but are just not disciplined enough to follow through. But if you knew the number of things that were fighting for your attention and soul, if you knew how beautifully bright the light at the end of the tunnel is, you would put in the work and not stop until it was finished. God requires discipline from you. He wants you to want it as much as He wants to give it to you.

Discipline is a key aspect of your healing journey. Why? Because the work you are about to do is not for a few months or years; it's for a lifetime. Every single day, you have to wake up and choose to leave the past in the past. It will be immensely hard, and God agrees with you.

The Bible says, *No discipline is enjoyable while it is happening—it's painful! But afterward there will be a peaceful harvest of right living for those who are trained in this way* (Hebrews 12:11, NLT). God knows the journey you are about to go through is a hard one, but He does promise that it's all for your good. This will be one of the hardest things you will ever do—you are literally fighting for your life here. But if God didn't think you could do it, He would not have kept you this long, and He would not have led you to this book.

Trust

Have you ever left your house to go to the grocery store without believing that you would get there or come back? You trust that the grocery store will be there. You trust that the canned beans will be in the aisle with the canned foods. You trust that if you can't immediately find what you need, you can ask someone to help you out. Isn't it strange how we put trust in the most mundane things, but when it comes to the things that matter, we do the opposite? We don't trust ourselves, and we don't trust God to come through like He said He would. Humans are a strange kind of being, aren't we?

Trust is earned, and perhaps you feel like you cannot trust God because He has not earned it. But He's earned it every single day of your life, in small and big ways. Every time you went to sleep and trusted that you would wake up, that was God waking you up.

Every time you went somewhere and came back safe and sound, that was God. Every time you sat in your kitchen and enjoyed a cup of coffee or relaxed in front of the TV watching Netflix or listened to music, that was God. You do realize there are millions of people in the world who are unable to do these simple things, right?

Your recovery is no trip to the grocery store. It's not sipping coffee and listening to music. No, it's a trip of a lifetime. I know you don't trust yourself to carry through, but that's okay. You don't have to. The one you need to trust with this journey is the one who's always been there, the one who without fail woke you up every morning. *God.* That's who you need to trust. He's earned it. He's more than earned it. So, take all that lack of trust in yourself, give it to God, and take the certainty that He gives.

You know why you need to trust God? Because again, this journey will be hard. God will require you to let go of everything, every direction and plan you had for yourself, and follow His plan for you. That's the biggest part of this journey. Along with staying disciplined and putting in the work, you have to trust that what you are doing is working, especially if you are doing it the way God wants you to. God implores us to trust Him in situations that seem to be taking too long or seem unfixable because He has seen the end. While you are in the beginning, pacing back and forth and biting your nails, God already sees you at peace in the end. It's why you need to *commit everything you do to the Lord. Trust him, and He will help you* (Psalm 37:5, NLT).

However, committing doesn't mean dumping your plans into God's hands and running off to do whatever pleases you. It doesn't mean putting in the work while doubting it will work. It means trusting wholeheartedly in the process God has set for you to follow. If you have no trust in something, your efforts in it will fall short, and you will struggle to stay disciplined. It's why you failed every single time you tried to do it yourself, because you had no trust in yourself to see it through and certainly no trust in God. It's also why the Bible says, *It is better to trust in the LORD than to put confidence in man* (Psalm 118:8, NLV). "Man" here includes you. Every step in chapters eight and nine is God-inspired. That's why the best way for them to work is to trust the One who inspired the steps.

When you truly begin your journey to healing, you will face obstacles and roadblocks, even from friends and family you expect to support you. Ironically, these obstacles and roadblocks may come in the way of "support." A friend may advise you not to create boundaries with your family because you might grow apart. Or a family member may tell you not to pay for therapy because it might not work, and you have more important bills to spend your money on. You will find that friend who encourages you to stay in that toxic relationship—what if you don't find someone who will love you again?

In those moments, you have to trust what God says about creating boundaries and not the childhood friend giving you misplaced advice. You have to trust that God will provide the money for your therapy and every other bill you have, because God gives us exactly what we need, when we need it. And you have to trust that you are loved, even when you are alone, even when you don't feel it. It's a lack of trust in God, in His plans and steps, that leads us astray, slows down our progress, and ruins our lives.

Trust your journey. Trust that the Author of your life has it all figured out, because He does.

Obey

Are you willing to obey what God tells you to do? This is a tough one. Many people don't factor God's directions into their day-to-day life. But if you are going to go from point A to B, you have to set aside what you think you know and obey what God is telling you to do. On your journey to healing, some of the things God will ask you to do will seem ludicrous. For instance God says to *respect and give thanks for those who try to bring bad to you. Pray for those who make it very hard for you* (Luke 6:28, NLV). Naturally, you are thinking, *Why would I want to pray for the mom or dad who abused me for years? Why should I bless them or forgive them?* It doesn't make sense; when someone hurts you, you want to find the best way to hurt them back. People will encourage you, even cheer you on, because you should never let someone who did something terrible to you go scot-free...

But God doesn't want you planning revenge; He's got it covered, and He's got a better plan than you could ever come up with. Be prepared, though, because when you obey God, people might look at you like you are a fool. But here's the thing about obeying God: there are rewards attached to it. Obeying God doesn't benefit Him in any way; honestly, He can do without you. Every time you obey God, all the benefits come to you. Luke 11:28 (NLV) supports this by saying, *Yes, but those who hear the Word of God and obey it are happy.* Happy—isn't that what we spend all our lives trying to be? Now, to think, we can achieve happiness by simply obeying God.

There are many stories in the Bible that show us just how blessed we become when we obey God:

The Wedding Feast at Cana (John 2:1-12)

The wedding had run out of wine. Wine! A very essential component at a wedding feast. Even if a wedding runs out of food for some reason, people always expect drinks to be available.

Jesus' mother, Mary, heard the servants grumbling, and at her urging, Jesus walked up to the servants and told them to fetch water into the empty jars. They didn't argue; they simply obeyed. At that point, they were desperate enough to try anything because there was nowhere else to get wine. You know the rest of the story: they filled the jars with water, and Jesus turned it into wine. They got the very best wine, all because they obeyed this man who spoke with authority and compassion.

You know what really gets me about this miracle? It was Jesus's first one! He hadn't performed any miracles that those servants could point to and say, "Hey, wasn't He the one who raised that girl from the dead? Sure, let's obey Him and pour water into the jars." They had nothing to go on about Jesus, and yet, they obeyed Him. We have so much to go on. We have proof and stories from people who cannot wait to tell about how amazing Jesus has been in their lives. So why do we find it hard to obey?

Simon's Many Fishes (Luke 5: 1-11 NIV)

Simon had been fishing all night and had come up with nothing. He was tired and had an empty net for all his troubles. Can you relate to this? Does this resonate every time you try to make your partner accept their lies and stop gaslighting you, or when you follow some Instagram influencer who promised to show you five steps to success and you come up empty?

When Jesus told Simon to cast his net into the sea, Simon was quick to point out he had done so all night and had caught nothing. He said, *Master, we've worked hard all night and haven't caught anything* (Luke 5:5,

NIV). But he added, *But because you say so, I will let down the nets* (Luke 5:5, NIV). His net filled up with fish almost immediately. It became so full that Simon had to call the other fishermen for help. He filled his boat and the boats of his partners. It was amazing, so amazing that Simon dropped to his knees and pleaded with Jesus to go away from him. *"Go away from me, Lord,"* he said, *"I am a sinful man!"* (Luke 5:8, NIV). But Jesus did not leave, because when God starts a blessing in your life, He doesn't leave it midway.

Do you know what gets me about this story? It's not just the fact that Simon obeyed despite all his wasted effort. That in itself was amazing. He had been fishing one way all night, but when Jesus told him to try again, He said to *put out into deep water* (Luke 5:4, NIV). Jesus knew Simon had been trying all night, so He said, now, try it my way, and Simon got two boats full of fish for obeying.

There are steps about your journey that you will not understand. They might sound foolish or unheard of, but when God tells you to do something, go ahead and do it. God cannot lead you astray; it is not in His nature.

God has given you the steps. He's shown you how to do the work. All He asks is that you trust Him. Are you going to obey?

CHAPTER 11

IF THEY COULD, SO CAN YOU

You *can* overcome your trauma and live an amazing life. Good can come out of despair, and many people have discovered this truth as well. Many celebrities have shared with the world their trauma from their adverse childhood experiences.

Celebrities such as Oprah Winfrey, Chevy Chase, Kelsey Grammer, Tyler Perry, and Jim Carrey, to name just a few, have gone through unspeakable traumas and come out on the other side of it, stronger and triumphant. But I'm not here to talk about these people. Their journeys are exceptional, and you can certainly learn and be inspired by reading about them. However, for now, I'd like to share some exceptional Bible characters. The Bible contains some of the greatest stories about trauma and redemption, and they are not talked about enough.

Joseph (Genesis 37-50, NIV)

The story of Joseph is probably one of the most popular in the Bible. You have no doubt heard it countless times in different settings. But let's bring Joseph's journey much closer to home.

Imagine yourself in Joseph's shoes: you are your father's favorite. He dotes on you, favors you over your eleven brothers, and gives you gifts without occasion or prompting. You love the attention; how could you not? How many other kids your age get to have a coat of many colors?

However, even though you love all the attention and gifts, you are aware of one unfortunate thing: your brothers hate you because of it. Joseph had to live with the discomfort of his father's favoritism every day, and it didn't help that, on top of being favored by his father, Joseph often brought bad reports to his father about his brothers. We don't know what these reports were, but the Bible doesn't say Joseph made them up. His brothers were far from perfect. He couldn't hang out with them without them spitefully pointing out one thing or another that their father had done for him. The Bible says, *When his brothers saw that their father loved him more than any of them, they hated him and could not speak a kind word to him* (Genesis 37:4, NIV). Imagine having all those siblings without any kind of caring relationship with them. It was terrible enough that Joseph had lost his mother, Rachel, at a very young age. Now he had to grow up in a house where the only family members who loved him were his father and younger brother, Benjamin. Suffice to say, it was an extremely traumatic situation. But that wasn't all Joseph would experience; there was even worse to come. His brothers hated him so much, they tried to kill him.

Imagine that it's a nice day out, and your father has sent you outside to check on your brothers. You put on your favorite coat, the one your father so lovingly gifted you. But when you get to where your brothers are, they are very unhappy to see you. The coat you are wearing becomes a symbol of their hate for you. The fact that their father loved you so much he gifted you something so exquisite, something he'd never thought to gift them before, troubles them. *Here comes that dreamer!* they said to each other. *Come now, let's kill him and throw him into one of these cisterns and say that a ferocious animal devoured him. Then we'll see what comes of his dreams* (Genesis 37:19 -20, NIV). Alarming, isn't it?

The brothers had every intention of murdering Joseph. The only reason Joseph was not killed immediately was that his older brother Reuben suggested that they throw him in the cistern and let the wilderness take care of him. Although, to be fair, Reuben did plan to come back, get him, and return him to their father. To buy himself time, he said, *Let's not take his life. Don't shed any blood. Throw him into this cistern here in the wilderness, but don't lay a hand on him* (Genesis 19:21-22, NIV). Imagine the terror Joseph must have felt, his own brothers about to murder him. You expect to feel safe with your family. You don't expect them to want to kill you. The brothers did throw Joseph into the cistern.

A cistern is an underground reservoir used for storing rainwater. The cistern Joseph's brothers threw him into was empty, cold, and dark. With eventual rainfall, unable to climb out, Joseph would have drowned. That's why Joseph's brothers listened to Reuben; even if they didn't kill him, he would most likely starve to death, and if he didn't, the rain would get him.

However, while Reuben was away, the brothers decided it would be a waste to kill Joseph, so they sold him to some Midianite slavers.

Joseph would go on to spend time in an Egyptian prison for two years for a rape crime he didn't commit. However, if Joseph had to recount the worst moment of his life, I'm sure he would go back to that time when his brothers almost murdered him but instead sold him into slavery.

Joseph suffered immensely. He dealt with hate and passive aggression from his siblings. He was almost murdered by the same siblings, he became a slave in a foreign land, and as if that was not enough, he was accused of a heinous crime. All the while, he was stuck in a foreign land wondering whether he would ever get to go home again. A home that wasn't exactly welcoming.

But here's one thing I need you to pick out from Joseph's story: God was with him through it all. When

Joseph got sold into slavery, God favored him before his master, so he put him in charge of everything in his household. When he was sent to prison, God favored him, so the warden put him in charge of the other prisoners. Joseph survived an attempted murder, slavery, and prison because God was with him. Even though his brothers, by selling him, thought they were getting rid of him, God was leading him straight to his destiny. A destiny He had equipped him for right from the very beginning, through the gift of being able to interpret dreams. God had seen—no, He *made*—Joseph's future, so He knew the world would need him.

You know how Joseph's story ends; he becomes the governor of Egypt, a position his very trauma had prepared him for. Because he had been a slave, because he had spent time in prison, being a governor humbled him. Through those experiences, he learned empathy, leadership, and kindness.

The things that happen to us don't just happen to us; we are nominated for them. Sometimes these terrible things happen to us so we can lead others; other times it's to serve as a testimony to others in a similar situation.

I'm certain there were times when Joseph was depressed. Being a slave would have exposed him to shame and robbed him of his self-worth and dignity. Being falsely accused of rape must have made him unable to trust people. I'm sure there was a time when he believed he was worthless, when he believed he had no place in the world. But the one thing Joseph did was to keep his mind centered. He never forgot where he came from, even when he had no idea where he was going. He never forgot the God of his fathers; if anything, his trauma drew him closer to God. Every time God needed Joseph to show up and trust Him, Joseph did. And because of that, Joseph saved Egypt and his family from starvation and death.

Despite how his father treated him, Joseph was not special. He was no more ordinary or extraordinary than you. It's even possible that you have gone through worse trauma than he did. Everything Joseph did was not by his power; it was through God's. So if he could turn his trauma into triumph, so can you.

Esther (Esther 1-10, NIV)

The book of Esther appears to be a romantic fairy tale, but on closer inspection, it's really not. Esther was a young woman who had to endure trauma from a very young age. She had lost her parents, and she and her uncle Mordecai were exiles in a foreign land. The Bible says, *Mordecai had a cousin named Hadassah, whom he had brought up because she had neither father nor mother. This young woman, who was also known as Esther, had a lovely figure and was beautiful. Mordecai had taken her as his own daughter when her father and mother died* (Esther 2:7, NIV).

Not only was Esther in exile in a foreign land, but she lived in an extremely patriarchal time. It was an era when girls were married off as young as fourteen, and women were often treated as little more than sexual objects. Yes, she had a cousin who loved and took care of her, but living in a time like this would no doubt have traumatized Esther. She was a very young lady whose freedom was severely limited by her gender while in exile in a land ruled by King Xerxes, a man who had no respect for God or people.

King Xerxes had banished his wife, Vashti, because she had refused to come out and display her considerable beauty before his all-male guests. Vashti declined to be objectified in front of the king's friends, leading the king, on the advice of his counsel, to remove her from her position and seek a new wife. Now, this is where the horror begins. He requested that every maiden of marriageable age be brought to his palace so he could choose a wife. Esther and millions of other girls were selected against their will. Mordecai had no choice but to let his little cousin go, but he was beside himself with worry because he knew exactly what was about to happen to the girls.

King Xerxes put the girls through six months of a beauty process, and then, to make his choice, he proceeded to bed a different one each night. Xerxes was essentially looking for a beautiful wife who could please him sexually and nothing else. This was a time when a woman's virginity was sacred, her worth directly tied to it. A non-virgin woman could not marry; she was considered defiled and, in most cases, had to grow old and die in her father's house. In Israel, the punishment for being an unmarried, non-virgin woman was death. (Deuteronomy 22:20-21)

Perhaps you've been sexually abused by someone in authority or who was supposed to protect you. So you wonder, why? Why does God allow this? Why does He leave power in the hands of people who abuse it? Why allow you or those millions of girls to go through what they went through? I wish I had the answer, but I don't. Only God does.

It is not a stretch to assume that Esther did not want to be there. She knew exactly what would happen to her if the king did not choose her.

Although barely a teenager, she would have to live the rest of her years alone and unmarried in her uncle's house. The possibility of trauma can be just as traumatizing as the trauma.

However, when it was Esther's turn, the king fell for her and made her his queen. But this is not a fairy tale ending, far from it. Esther may have been a queen, but she had to make a special request just to see her husband. If she approached him at an unpermitted time, he could have her killed.

Everything Esther went through led her to that moment. God wanted to use her to prevent the genocide of her people. The Bible says that Esther had a lovely figure and was beautiful, which might have played a role in the king choosing her. But when it came to saving her people, her beauty and figure had nothing to do with it. Instead, it was her God-given wisdom. No one else could have averted the genocide of the Jews the way she did. In a land of powerful and ruthless men, God used Esther to accomplish what none of them could, all while being the queen to a king who did not hold women in high regard. You could say she did it amidst a traumatic, stressful situation. Being a queen did not exempt Esther from the threat of death along with the Jews, as in their eyes, she was a Jew first before anything else.

When her cousin first told her of the plot to kill the Jews and that she was the only one who could help, Esther was terrified. She sent her cousin a message to let him know that there was nothing she could do. She said, *All the king's officials and the people of the royal provinces know that for any man or woman who approaches the king in the inner court without being summoned the king has but one law: that they be put to death unless the king extends the gold scepter to them and spares their lives. But thirty days have passed since I was called to go to the king* (Esther, 4:10, NIV).

Mordecai heard this and was quick to remind her that being the queen didn't make her special. If the Jews were killed, she would be killed along with them. He said, *Do not think that because you are in the king's house you alone of all the Jews will escape. For if you remain silent at this time, relief and deliverance for the Jews will arise from another place, but you and your father's family will perish. And who knows but that you* have come to your royal position for such a time as this? (Esther, 4:12-14, NIV).

Mordecai hated to put her in this situation, but he had no choice. And Esther, with her heart in her stomach, said, *Go, gather together all the Jews who are in Susa, and fast for me. Do not eat or drink for three days, night or day. I and my attendants will fast as you do. When this is done, I will go to the king, even though it is against the law. And if I perish, I perish* (Esther 4:16, NIV).

You see, the thing about Esther's story is that her trauma doesn't look like trauma, but it was. She had already experienced the trauma of losing her parents, and now she faced the looming trauma of the possible death of herself and her people. But everything she went through, from losing her parents to being in exile and getting chosen by the king, led her to that moment. Remember Mordecai's words? He said, *And who knows but that you have come to your royal position for such a time as this?* (Esther 4:14, NIV).

Maybe, like Esther, your trauma doesn't look like trauma. Perhaps you grew up in a wealthy home, with privileges that most people don't have, so others don't expect you to complain or acknowledge any traumas. They have minimized your trauma to something nonexistent, and that has made it all the more overwhelming for you.

But consider the situation Esther was in. She was an orphan, forced to marry a king and become a queen who had to watch her every step. She had no voice and no say in what happened to her or how it did. Yet, with God's help, she saved an entire race of people.

If Esther could do it, if she could take her situation and turn it into an opportunity, then so can you.

CHAPTER 12

YOU ARE GOD'S MASTERPIECE

For we are God's masterpiece. He has created us anew in Christ Jesus, so we can do the good things he planned for us long ago. (Ephesians 2:10, NLT)

Dear Reader,

The Oxford dictionary describes a masterpiece as a work of "outstanding artistry, skill, or workmanship." That's a fine definition, but it doesn't even begin to come close to God's description of the masterpiece that you are.

For one, we are not just a masterpiece. We are not just a fine work of art to be valued, because in Christ, our value appreciates over time. We never go out of fashion, we never depreciate, we never lose our value.

Rather, we grow, we change, and we become anew.

Do you understand what it means to become anew? It means all the old, bad things in your life don't matter anymore. Your slate's been wiped clean, and you, with God's help, get to rewrite your story, the story He meant for you to live all along. You no longer have to live by your hurt, your trauma, your sin, or the flaws the world is so quick to point out. You no longer have to indulge it. It's ceased to matter because you have been created anew.

I know you don't see it, and I know you are struggling to believe it. Being a masterpiece feels unreal and untrue to you. You are thinking, how can you, with your many flaws, sins, and trauma, be a masterpiece? What about all the things you've done? All the mistakes you've made? All the hurt you've endured? What about the fact that people have tagged you a victim; unfixable and damaged?

I know there are days when you wake up and are too tired to get out of bed. I know there are days when you can't bear to look in the mirror because you are afraid of what you'll see. I know that on the days when you do look in the mirror, you hate what you see. I know there are days when the burden of your trauma feels heavier, tougher, and insurmountable. I know you've gone all your life hearing the same words; you aren't good enough, strong enough, pretty enough, or smart enough.

These words have been cut into your body, and they hurt. You don't feel like a masterpiece. You feel tired, broken, ashamed, small, and unloved.

But think of yourself as a thousand-year-old, priceless painting. In the hands of anyone else, you are just old and damaged. But in the hands of a restorer, or an art enthusiast, you are a rare gem, a masterpiece. That's how you are in the eyes of God. In the eyes of the world, your mother, your father, or even yourself, you are damaged and broken. But in God's eyes, you are the most unique and beautiful thing to ever exist. That's what God sees when He looks at you, and it's okay if right now you don't see it. All you have to do is accept it. Acceptance brings clarity. Acceptance brings renewal.

God has never looked at you as damaged or broken. God never thought you were unlovable or unforgivable. God doesn't think of you as weak. How could He think that when He made you in His image and called you by name? When His strength is yours whenever you need it?

Do you know the amazing thing about being God's masterpiece? He does not expect you to be or think of you as perfect. He takes away that burden of having to be and do everything right. He knows it's impossible. He knows there are days when you feel like an overwrung dishcloth or a used tissue. He knows about your off days before they even happen.

He knows you are going to hurt. He knows you will hurt people and make mistakes. He knows that on your journey to renewal, you will fall off the wagon more times than you care to admit, and yet, He still sees and thinks of you as a masterpiece.

God thinks of you as a creature worthy of love, respect, and acceptance. As a person who can move and break mountains. As a woman who is a force to be reckoned with; as a man who can lead and instruct. He thinks of you as an inventor, a lover, a forgiver. As a light that leads others to even more light. To God, you are and can be the light at the end of the tunnel for that person who needs it, regardless of where you are now. You can be the best at your job, the mother your child needs, the daughter your parents need, the influencer and leader the world is looking for. To God, you were formed for a purpose that's not just unique but also merges and supports the purpose of others. To God, your strength is not physical or mental; it has to do with Him because He gives you the strength you will need. He always has.

Perhaps you don't fully understand how amazing you are. Let me break it down for you:

In God's eyes, you are not just a masterpiece; you are His temple, and His Spirit dwells in you (1 Corinthians 3:16). God's Spirit isn't one of timidity. God's Spirit isn't broken or flawed; it is the balm that heals all brokenness. God is not a God who leaves His temple damaged. He fixes and makes new what He creates, as many times as you need Him to.

In the eyes of God, you are a *chosen people. You are royal priests, a holy nation, God's very own possession. As a result, you can show others the goodness of God, for he called you out of the darkness into his wonderful light* (1 Peter 2:9, NLT). In God's eyes, you are chosen—chosen for His goodness and chosen to show others His goodness. There's nothing random about you. Even when you feel like a mistake, you are not one—you are God's possession, and those whom God owns, He protects, preserves, and blesses. He is a Creator who delights in His work and spends His time perfecting it. And that work, that masterpiece, is you.

In the eyes of God, *you are the light of the world* (Matthew 5:14, NLT). Regardless of the darkness you feel, to God, you are and have always been created to be a light—a warm, beautiful light. God thinks so highly of you, so warmly, so lovingly. He is always fixing and refining you, always reshaping and remolding. God has an intense, bottomless, overwhelming love for you. And He doesn't love you because you are a masterpiece; He loves you because you are His child. He loves you for all the things you are not and all the things you will be. Even in the moments when you weren't aware, He was there fixing and directing. He is the reason you survived as long as you did. He is the reason your heart is changing and renewing. He is the reason the journey to the other side of your trauma will be an amazing success. All your life, without knowing who you were or what you were created for, you sought validation from all the wrong places. You were robbed of the masterpiece that you are, and the people of the world trampled on your uniqueness. Well, God is restoring that. You never stopped being valuable to God. You never stopped being His treasured possession, His precious temple. You never stopped being His masterpiece. So, take off the lies that the enemy has clothed you with and go be what God made you to be all along: an exquisite masterpiece.

Much Love,
Shyra.

REFERENCES

Bible References

All Scripture marked NIV is taken from Holy Bible, New International Version®, NIV® Copyright ©1973, 1978, 1984, 2011 by Biblica, Inc.® Used by permission. All rights reserved worldwide.

All Scripture marked NLT is taken from Holy Bible, New Living Translation, copyright © 1996, 2004, 2015 by Tyndale House Foundation. Used by permission of Tyndale House Publishers, Inc., Carol Stream, Illinois 60188. All rights reserved.

All Scripture marked NLV is taken from New Life Version (NLV) Copyright © 1969, 2003 by Barbour Publishing, Inc.

All Scripture marked NRSVA is taken from New Revised Standard Version Bible: Anglicized Edition, copyright © 1989, 1995 the Division of Christian Education of the National Council of the Churches of Christ in the United States of America. Used by permission. All rights reserved

Articles

Daniel R Weinberger. (2018, June 28). *Extreme Stress in Childhood Is Toxic to Your DNA.* https://theconversation.com/extreme-stress-in-childhood-is-toxic-to-your-dna-99009

Dan Matthews, CPRP. (n.d.) *How to Identify Your Limiting Beliefs and Get Over Them.* https://www.lifehack.org/858652/limiting-beliefs

Fast Facts: *Preventing Adverse Childhood Experiences. (2022, April 6). Centers for Disease Control and Prevention.* https://www.cdc.gov/violenceprevention/aces/fastfact.html

Herzog & Schmahl. (2018, September 4). *Adverse Childhood Experiences and the Consequences on Neurobiological, Psychosocial, and Somatic Conditions Across the Lifespan.* https://www.ncbi.nlm.nih.gov/pmc/articles/PMC6131660/#:~:text=Results%3A%20In%20adulthood%2C%20the%20history,personality%20disorder%2C%20obesity%20and%20diabetes.

Kyle Bowe. (2019, June 5). *Your Odds of Being Alive.* https://medium.com/afwp/your-odds-of-being-alive-af7826915073

The Science of ACEs and Toxic Stress. (2022). *ACEs Aware.* https://www.acesaware.org/ace-fundamentals/the-science-of-aces-toxic-stress/

Understanding Child Trauma. (2022, September 9). *Substance Abuse and Mental Health Services Administration.* https://www.samhsa.gov/child-trauma/understanding-child-trauma

Vaidis & Bran. (2020, October 28). *Cognitive Dissonance Theory.* https://www.oxfordbibliographies.com/display/document/obo-9780199828340/obo-9780199828340-0156.xml#:~:text=The%20theory%20of%20cognitive%20dissonance,%2C%20the%20cognitive%20dissonance%20state).

Shyra Smith

4 Ways That Adverse Childhood Experiences Affect Adults. (2022, November, 29). *Better Help.* https://www.betterhelp.com/advice/childhood/4-ways-that-adverse-childhood-experiences-affect-adults/

www.ingramcontent.com/pod-product-compliance
Lightning Source LLC
Chambersburg PA
CBHW040742060526
44119CB00075B/208